THE LONELINESS
EPIDEMIC

THE LONELINESS EPIDEMIC

*Why So Many of Us Feel Alone—
and How Leaders Can Respond*

Susan Mettes

Foreword by DAVID KINNAMAN

Brazos Press
a division of Baker Publishing Group
Grand Rapids, Michigan

© 2021 by Susan Mettes

Published by Brazos Press
a division of Baker Publishing Group
PO Box 6287, Grand Rapids, MI 49516-6287
www.brazospress.com

Printed in the United States of America

Library of Congress Cataloging-in-Publication Data
Names: Mettes, Susan, 1980– author.
Title: The loneliness epidemic : why so many of us feel alone—and how leaders can respond / Susan Mettes ; foreword by David Kinnaman.
Description: Grand Rapids, Michigan : Brazos Press, a division of Baker Publishing Group, [2021]
Identifiers: LCCN 2021011632 | ISBN 9781587434778 (cloth) | ISBN 9781493432769 (ebook)
Subjects: LCSH: Loneliness—Religious aspects—Christianity.
Classification: LCC BV4911 .M48 2021 | DDC 259—dc23
LC record available at https://lccn.loc.gov/2021011632

Baker Publishing Group publications use paper produced from sustainable forestry practices and post-consumer waste whenever possible.

21 22 23 24 25 26 27   7 6 5 4 3 2 1

To Serge and Lazarus

CONTENTS

FOREWORD

DAVID KINNAMAN

On June 5, 2017, my life changed in an instant. My wife, Jill, checked herself into the hospital for a debilitating migraine. A few hours later, she texted me that a medical scan revealed a massive brain tumor. That day began a crazy-hard journey that has fundamentally shaped my understanding of loneliness.

I suppose I'd felt lonely before that, but the past four years brought me to the deepest places of anguish, as my high school sweetheart and wife of twenty-five years passed away in late 2020 after a heroic, faith-filled battle with brain cancer. At times, I've felt desperate, aching loneliness.

My crisis of loneliness was precipitated by the diagnosis and eventual death of Jill. Yet millions upon millions of people experience loneliness in our society in all sorts of ways and due to all sorts of factors.

To be crystal clear, loneliness is an intricately complex subject that is not at all the same thing as being alone, feeling sad or depressed, or simply being unmarried (which is a common misperception among Christian leaders). Ironically, some of the loneliest experiences can take place while you're surrounded by other people.

So what makes people lonely? What are the undercurrents and forces creating a lonelier society? And how can Christian communities better minister to the lonely? In this fantastic book, behavioral scientist and researcher—and, I am honored to say, my good friend!—Susan Mettes helps us get beneath the surface of these and other crucial questions.

Loneliness is multifaceted, and it has reached epidemic proportions. Consider these examples, based on research from our team at Barna Group:

- One in three adults in the United States (36%) say they feel lonely almost all the time or sometimes.
- The proportion of adults who say they could be accurately described as lonely has more than doubled in the span of just over twenty-five years, from 7 percent in 1994 to 12 percent in 2002 and to 20 percent in our most recent tracking.
- In research Barna conducted for the Boone Center for the Family at Pepperdine University, one in five Americans (22%) say they experience unwanted singleness that affects their most significant relationships. What's more, nearly half of all practicing Christian Millennials (43%) say they experience unwanted singleness.
- Based on research we conducted in twenty-five countries and nine languages for World Vision, we found that one in four 18- to 35-year-olds around the world (23%) said they feel "lonely and isolated from others." Furthermore, only one in three (32%) indicated that "someone believes in me."
- If loneliness zoomed to crisis levels before 2020, it has even more importance in the wake of the mental health

challenges wrought by the global pandemic. But as you will see in original research Barna conducted with Susan Mettes, rates of loneliness were unexpectedly flat through the first year of the pandemic. Still, young adults, people who feel insecure, and even people who want more privacy feel intense loneliness these days. Nor are churchgoers immune.

The fact that the United States has such widespread loneliness means that we have widespread problems with relationships. To have better relationships in our households, neighborhoods, and organizations, we need to address loneliness: individually and collectively.

It's not all doom and gloom, though. There are proactive, tangible ways forward.

For one thing, the subject of loneliness is no longer taboo. Let's acknowledge the positive development that we can better understand and talk about loneliness today than at any time before. I happen to believe it's a good thing people are so willing to be honest about their emotions and self-perceptions, even in the context of anonymous survey research. As you'll see in this book, Millennials and Gen Z are especially open about mental and emotional health topics and are also dealing with anxiety and loneliness at higher-than-average levels. Their candor on these topics should be another indicator that the time is ripe for richer explanations and better solutions to loneliness. (And, yes, social media makes relationships and connections challenging, but it can—surprisingly!—actually play a positive role in alleviating loneliness.)

My team at Barna was privileged to work with Susan on this project, which has implications for so many people, for church leaders, and for our society. We thought research was the right way to approach this topic because we need to hear from lonely people themselves rather than guessing at what their experience is. At the outset, Susan explained to me that she wanted readers to understand other people better, and my hope is that this book will serve as encouragement that we can do something about loneliness.

I have worked alongside Susan on numerous projects with Barna Group over the years. I am especially grateful for her careful, nuanced, and biblical approach to problems, as she demonstrates here in this important book. In the writing process, Susan talked about wanting to stamp out stereotypes— that the lonely must be old and isolated, for example. Many people think we should have happy hours in retirement homes to address loneliness. In fact, people who are young are more likely to be lonely.

Susan offers meaningful ways the church can minister to lonely people, going far beyond simplistic solutions to addressing their inner lives and the God who understands them. If you're experiencing loneliness or know someone who is—or if you work in churches, schools, companies, or organizations where there are human beings (yes, that's pretty much all of us)—you should know what ideas are circulating about the crush of loneliness and the buffering of healthy relationships. Susan helps us to close these gaps.

In my own journey of bereavement and loneliness, Susan's work has helped. With the assistance of her valuable insights, I strive each day toward greater connection with God, with others, and with my soul.

ACKNOWLEDGMENTS

This book, as I've recently learned all books are, was a team effort.

Thanks to my husband, Serge, who relinquished much of the time we would have spent together to the book, who helped me talk through its ideas, and who has been a huge support throughout. I will always remember that extra night we had in Tanzania, when we sat under the trees and dreamed up this project.

Thanks to the team at Barna, particularly Pam Jacob, Brooke Hempell, and Daniel Copeland, who did the detailed and essential work to run the surveys I used in this book, as well as getting me the results. Many thanks also to David Kinnaman and Brenda Usery, whose trust and investment made this book possible.

To Mom, who has been my first reader throughout my life, thank you for your insight and feedback. And thank you, Dad; your support and enthusiasm encouraged me and helped me see that this was possible.

Thank you to all I interviewed for this project, including Greg Scheer, Dick Thompson, Ryan Frederick, Scott G. Frickenstein,

Andy Crouch, Linford Detweiler, Matt Jenson, Stephanie Holmer, Caelene Peake, Sharon Hargrave, Sanyin Siang, Sandra Van Opstal, and Brooke Hempell. It's good to be on a highly remote team with you, working to bring about human flourishing as humans seem increasingly willing to forgo it. Blessings on your work.

Thanks to my editor and former colleague, Katelyn Beaty, who took a chance on a first-time author and whose work is always worth reading.

I wrote almost all of this book bouncing on an exercise ball, with my baby asleep in a carrier. It was not how I'd planned for his naps or my writing to go. But thanks to Rain for Roots for producing some of the only songs that would put him to sleep and didn't drive me insane when played four or five times in a row.

Thanks to Lazarus and to God for the perspective that babies give: God has made people inexpressibly wonderful, from their first moments on. He designed relationships to be more worthwhile than any accomplishment, as I quickly remembered whenever I looked down and saw my son's four-toothed smile. I hope some of my awe and gratefulness has come through so that you readers can share it. I'm thankful to you too.

Part 1

UNDERSTANDING AN EPIDEMIC

1

LONELY AMERICANS

Studying Our Loneliness

I can't remember at what point I realized that I would probably go two years without a hug. Nobody knew how much worse the pandemic would get, but I knew I would be stuck in place for the duration. My friends felt a world away. Phone calls with my family had become strained. I couldn't tell how they were really doing or articulate how I was handling the stress. The fact is I had stopped showering altogether, and I was watching the Lord of the Rings movies repeatedly.

I believe winter was approaching when the realization about huglessness hit me. Holidays loomed in the near future, and I wondered if I could deal with a Thanksgiving by myself, with horse meat instead of turkey.

I was in Central Asia. It was 2004.

That period, when I was a Peace Corps volunteer, was one of my deepest experiences of loneliness. I was in a community where only one person I knew spoke English well. I could talk on a pay phone with people in the United States—through a very bad connection where I could always hear a third person breathing on the line—once every two weeks. I got sick a lot. I didn't bathe much since the Turkish bathhouse was open to women just one day a week, during a time when I was scheduled to teach. People I didn't know would come to my house to ask me to help them cheat on their English tests. I started talking to myself.

But there were bright spots. On Sunday nights the main television station would air Jackie Chan movies. I watched them with my tiny sixty-something landlady/roommate. We would sit next to each other on the floor cushions, and she would slap my knee during the funniest parts. Laughing at the same thing with another human was like gulping down chocolate milk after a hard run.

It dawned on me that my students were lonely too. They had come to a boarding school with Dickensian meals and discipline, and they missed their families. So I designed a class or two based on the Townes Van Zandt song "If I Needed You," covered by Emmylou Harris. It was good teaching material because it used the subjunctive mood properly, but I mostly played it because it felt good. Like many of the Bible passages on loneliness, the song doesn't use the word *lonely* or *loneliness*, but we all knew the underlying meaning.

> If I needed you, would you come to me?
> Would you come to me for to ease my pain?

The song connected with me and my students because it was a cry to someone we trusted, a cry of vulnerability, a cry for belongingness and to be taken care of in our low moments. In the song, someone answers that cry. In our real lives at the time, the answer was *wait*.

My students and I are not the only ones to look to music and art when we feel most lonesome. Linford Detweiler and Karin Bergquist are a husband-and-wife team who have made dozens of albums in their twenty-five-plus years as part of the band Over the Rhine. Widely respected for the beauty of their lyrics and music, Over the Rhine is among the groups that seem to be assigned to a different genre with each album they put out.

As Bergquist once said when kicking off a 2019 concert near Washington, DC, "We're going to bring you down. It's what we do best." Their music is emotionally complex, and much of it is undeniably lonesome. Detweiler told me, "Karin and I have often referred to songs as 'safe containers for pain.' Songs can hold something for you (both the writer and the listener) and, in so doing, help you release something heavy that maybe you don't want to carry around every day. The song will do the heavy lifting for you."[1]

Is that why it felt good to listen to music about loneliness when I felt lonely? Detweiler affirms that there can be a cathartic effect. He says, "I don't necessarily understand it, but 'lonely' songs can make us feel less alone, like we are seen, like others have been there too."[2]

In fact, the song "If I Needed You" still whisks me back fifteen years to a daybed in a little room on a steppe where Scythians' horses had grazed, where I sat smelling like sweaty wool and writing long letters in Word XP.

And it turned out well enough. Some of my prayers for hugs were answered in the form of packages. The bird flu pandemic resulted in a few hundred deaths but was brought under control. I made a local friend or two. I acquired a taste for horse and was able to celebrate holidays with my wonderfully warm, funny house church.

In 2020, when the COVID-19 pandemic hit the United States—killing hundreds of thousands—millions of people were stuck at home and feeling the way I did when I thought I would not get a hug for two years.

Or were they?

More than one survey revealed that people in the United States did not feel more lonely months into the pandemic and social isolation than they had before. What can explain this? And what explains the rise in loneliness in the years leading up to that point?

Why, when we have so many means of communication and getting close to each other, are we more lonely than ever recorded? Why did we seem to stop getting lonelier just when our ability to connect in person shut off suddenly?

The answers lie in a few themes woven through the chapters that follow: belonging, security, expectations, and closeness.

The Research

Most of the statistics in this book come from two surveys conducted by Barna Group as part of their OmniPoll series.[3] People could take these surveys online. Just over one thousand participants completed the first survey between February 18 and March 4, 2020. Throughout the book, when I write "in the winter of 2020," the data comes from that survey. This represents a more normal time in the lives of Americans, so I use it often for more generalized statements about Americans' loneliness. One thousand participants completed the second survey between April 28 and May 11, 2020. Throughout the book, when I write "in the spring of 2020," the data comes from that survey.

Data scientists at Barna weighted the results from the two surveys so that the proportion in age, ethnicity, education level, region, and gender would match the proportion of Americans in those groups, allowing for better extrapolation. There's reasonable certainty that if a different group of US adults took the surveys over again, the statistics we'd get would be about the same—within a few points of the winter and spring 2020 surveys.

A third, earlier Barna study looked at young adults around the world. This is the Connected Generation report.[4] Since this applies only to young people, I don't refer to it as often. However, it has some fascinating insights about differences in how young people around the world feel.[5]

Statisticians and researchers have to look at a number of factors to decide what the data is saying—and whether it's worth talking about. In this book, I try to report differences that have a very low likelihood of being accidental (that is, they're statistically significant) and are also big enough in magnitude to make a noticeable difference in life.

Intuition is a wonderful gift for a researcher. However, intuition should never stand untested. Without quantitative results, we'd never know whether it was our assumptions or a real understanding of people that led us to our conclusions.

Barna Group has been studying and interviewing people for decades, and their research brings people's actual thoughts and experiences to the table, rather than researchers' guesses at them. A key part of what Barna and I did was to ask questions that would confirm or deny that my educated guesses about loneliness were accurate. Some were and some weren't.

Loneliness is difficult to measure and compare from person to person because it's subjective. People who say they feel lonely are lonely. And sometimes people who don't say they feel lonely are lonely too.

To study loneliness, we can use a number of techniques to try to get reliable information on loneliness in big groups. We can ask people how often they feel lonely, how lonely they feel, when they feel lonely, and how long they have felt lonely. We can also ask indirectly about loneliness. One often-used battery of questions, the UCLA Loneliness Scale, uses this technique. The questions include "How much of the time do you feel you lack companionship? How much of the time do you feel left out? How much of the time do you feel that you are 'in tune' with other people?"[6] The scale asks people to answer with responses like "often," "sometimes," "rarely," or "never."

Asking people to say whether they felt lonely often, sometimes, rarely, or never leaves us with yet another very subjective measure, and it's hard to draw conclusions when one person's "often" may be weekly and another's may be daily. So, in the Barna studies, I asked respondents how often they had felt lonely in the past week and allowed them to select a specific, yet not too specific, time frame ("not daily but during at least one day"). In this book, when I talk about the frequency of loneliness in the Barna studies, it's based on answers to that question.

In addition, I asked those who had felt lonely in the past week how painful their loneliness was, giving a seven-point scale and guidelines at the bottom ("barely noticeable"), middle ("intense"), and top ("unbearable") of the scale. When I talk about the intensity or pain of loneliness, I'm talking about answers to that question.

In the course of the research, when I looked on as focus groups discussed something and as I read the conclusions of the researchers I cite here, I felt a ping of wonder and affection for people. How amazing that we form bonds so easily! That we give each other so many chances! That we are willing to endure so many sorts of unpleasantness for the sake of relationships and people we care for!

And usually, I also experienced twinges of frustration. Why do people fail to take care of themselves and of others in ways that would be so simple? Why say and believe things that are obviously untrue?

People are indeed wonderful and frustrating. Moses knew it, and so did Jesus. Both of them had a sort of unrequited (or under-requited) love and the desire to save people who didn't want what was good for them. Addressing social problems often comes with this tension. Like other social problems, loneliness is often rooted in people making decisions and forming habits that work against their good.

This book is for helping Christian leaders understand the landscape of loneliness, how to encourage others, and how to lead a community that deals well with the threat and the fact of loneliness. Loneliness is something to be understood and, if possible, transformed into belonging. How do we transform loneliness? How do we help others transform their loneliness? Many of the answers lie in long-term processes.

I cannot offer complete solutions. You will not be curing American loneliness after reading this book. Hopefully, however, you will know how to prevent it, recognize it, defang it, and help others do the same.

Writing about Loneliness in 2020

In 2020, the topic of loneliness was everywhere. Concern for seniors in retirement homes, for singles stuck in efficiency apartments, and for other groups of Americans rose as it became clear that the disease could overwhelm hospitals and interfere with care. Keeping the most vulnerable people safe became a priority, and that meant keeping our lives to ourselves.

What Americans of every stripe experienced combines several factors that contribute to loneliness: rejection, discrimination, and the suspicion that one's neighbors wouldn't help in an emergency. Put another way, they show a breakdown in belongingness, the warm network of mutually trusting and important relationships.

Although loneliness was a hot topic in 2020, it is by no means a new feature of American life. I started writing this book before the COVID-19 pandemic. The topic seemed timely, and when the US surgeon general declared loneliness a national epidemic, I had already been seeing loneliness lurking in the Barna data.

In addition to articles expressing concern about the rise of loneliness, there are the answering voices saying it has often been like this. In the book *In Search of Intimacy: Surprising Conclusions from a Nationwide Survey on Loneliness and What to Do about It*, Carin Rubenstein and Phillip Shaver say, "Some experts have begun referring to the new 'nationwide epidemic of loneliness.' But even back in the 1940s, journalist John Gunther, traveling all over the country to research his book on America, called loneliness 'one of the supreme American problems.'"[7] *In Search of Intimacy* was published in 1982, and it has the smell and the curlicue script lettering to prove it.

Rates of loneliness are higher today than they were in the 1980s, when they were already high enough to alarm cultural commentators, but we should note that loneliness is a chronic problem. Especially when we expect quick fixes, chronic problems can seem like something fresh going wrong. Yet in the 1850s, the 1940s, the 1980s, and the 2020s, cultural commentators sounded the alarm about American loneliness. Here's hoping that in the 2030s they start discussing its decline.

We know very little about loneliness in the United States. We know what is happening now, of course, but we don't have much data from the past. We don't know what loneliness was like for America's slaves. We don't know what loneliness was like for American pioneers. We don't know what loneliness was like for our troops in World War II. We don't know what loneliness was like for the first Chinese immigrants to California. We don't know what loneliness was like for Native Americans before Europeans ever arrived.

The statistical studies that allow us to compare loneliness in America between the last few decades and today didn't exist for other times when we might have expected a good deal of loneliness. But expected and reported loneliness are very different. One of the main findings of this book is that groups of people often disprove our hypotheses about their levels of loneliness.

If we had survey data on groups throughout American history, we might be surprised. They may have given us insight into how to help our society now.

What we experience is a blip in history—and yet we have reason to believe that we could connect with generations going back to the beginning, when Adam couldn't find a suitable companion. We believe that loneliness could help us connect even across cultures.

Loneliness is something that people have experienced, as far as we can tell, in all times and places. Loneliness is perennial. Loneliness is pretty much universal. And yet loneliness is urgent.

America's Loneliness Problem

That said, loneliness seems to have an upside. Think of much of American music, from B. B. King to Billie Eilish. Would it really be a good thing to erase the loneliness behind their music? Would we prefer that Fyodor Dostoevsky or Charlie Chaplin hadn't understood disappointment and isolation?

Along these lines, some question whether we should try to solve loneliness. They propose that it has a place in human flourishing. I cautiously agree. Occasional loneliness is a foil to satisfying relationships. Thirsting for them every now and then might make us better at investing in intimacy.

However, chronic loneliness is defined by deficiency and distress, and it has destructive effects on human life and creativity. Chronic loneliness is rooted in unquenchable insecurity. Such loneliness pushes people toward death, senility, heart trouble, and poor responses to disease. These are not good things; we shouldn't encourage each other to just live with them throughout a shortened life. To be sure, our bodies and minds need unexpected challenges and even painful ones. Many Christians would say we need stress for spiritual development. But we also need rest from stress for physical healing, for problem solving, and—yes—for spiritual development. That means we need relief from loneliness, at least for periods of time.

America Has an Intimacy Problem

For our loneliness problem to transform, our culture needs transformation.

One reason for our loneliness is that intimacy in America is sick. Intimacy is part of the recipe for satisfying relationships. In money matters—one of the most private aspects of Americans' lives—intimacy is upended. Almost a third of Millennials have joint bank accounts before marriage,[8] but a similar proportion of married Millennials (28%) don't have joint accounts with their spouses.[9]

Americans seem to have fewer trusted relationships than they used to. In 2006, researchers at Duke found that the number of people Americans had important conversations with dropped from three in 1985 to two in 2006. It gets worse: a quarter of Americans said they had no one to talk to about "important matters."[10]

In other words, we are more likely to share our bodies than our thoughts and concerns. Needless to say, this is all backward and inside out. People are designed to be relationship-makers and designed to share friendship and emotional intimacy far more broadly than sex. It's as if we decided to walk on our hands all the time; we might get pretty good at it, but it's still a bad idea. We've set ourselves up not only for loneliness but also for spiritual injury.

Sharon Hargrave is the executive director of the Boone Center for the Family. She has been a therapist for more than thirty years. She says that "intimacy in our society has been defined more as need-meeting," an error that steers us further from what it can actually be, causing us to eliminate relationships that are unsatisfying rather than address problems with the teamwork that comes with real intimacy.[11]

But this isn't where the crisis of American intimacy ends: we have a crisis of friendship. In the 2006 study, people were more likely to drop nonfamilial relationships from their list of trusted confidants, leaving spouses and parents to bear more of the burden of our needs for important conversations.[12] Many readers will be familiar with Robert Putnam's research in *Bowling Alone*, now two decades old, which showed a dramatic decline in social engagement among Americans, including a 43 percent drop in family dinners and a 58 percent drop in attending club meetings.[13]

These small networks can become echo chambers, as we tend to select people like ourselves to talk with about important things. When people in groups already share perspectives, the echo can get louder and more distorted.[14] We need people who are different from us to weigh in on important issues.

In this book, I'll argue that we need to correct for this by investing more heavily in friendships than in family. That's countercultural, but there's good research behind it. Researchers discovered that chosen rather than kin relationships tend to help us most with loneliness.[15] That is, the people we meet and become friends with often matter more to our loneliness than parents or siblings. This may seem strange—what relationship has more potential than what we have with parents or siblings? The reason isn't clear from research so far, but one possibility is that deep friendships take a different kind of investment and produce a different kind of experience. The ability to make and keep friendships is essential to human flourishing. As wonderful as family is, it's time we started deepening relationships with those who aren't related to us.

Loneliness and the Church

Given the scale of loneliness, what can Christian leaders do?

The church already does many of the things that address loneliness. Some of these are even things that doctors might be prescribing post-pandemic, like group singing (which makes people feel happier and closer),[16] community service, being part of a community that meets in person, providing confidants/confessors, and having people you can call on in an emergency. But the church is not essentially a collection of activities that benefit mental health. We worship a real God who is a being we can know now—and whom we will meet soon.

There is a real danger of letting positive psychology hijack the church's real purpose. It is because of what the Christian faith teaches that Christians do so many things that are good for loneliness. But confronting loneliness isn't an ultimate goal. In the taxonomy of church priorities, it is a subcategory of loving your neighbor.

If we aim only to reduce loneliness, we will miss. Instead, we should consider an investment of attention, naming and talking about loneliness as we aim at godliness, neighbor love, hospitality, and peace. Don't be fooled into thinking that will be easy. The church has a loneliness problem in more than one sense.

First, there is widespread loneliness in the church. In the winter of 2020, about one in six people (16%) who attend church regularly said they are lonely all the time. A majority were lonely at some point in any week. Second, there is a greater stigma attached to loneliness among practicing Christians than among other faith groups. More practicing Christians than nonpracticing Christians or non-Christians said loneliness is always (rather than sometimes or never) embarrassing. A quarter of practicing Christians (25%) said loneliness is always bad, making them more likely than nonpracticing Christians and non-Christians to say so. We often conflate feeling bad with sin, despite knowing that Jesus was "a man of sorrows" (Isa. 53:3).

There are gaps in our Christian lives that demonstrate an inability to transform loneliness into belonging. For example, almost a third of Christian households barely, if ever, practice hospitality. Only 60 percent have guests to their homes once a month, and only 39 percent have guests who aren't family members.[17] In an intimacy-starved society, shouldn't Christians be open enough to have people over every now and then?

It's time the church took ministry for mental health, including loneliness, more seriously. Churches should spend at least the amount of energy to address loneliness as they do to get meals to new parents. Loneliness is a less simple burden, but we are to carry one another's burdens nevertheless.

Loneliness around the World

The United States is not the only country having a loneliness crisis. While there is little data on loneliness in countries with lower gross domestic product, there is a lot of data on countries that are similar in wealth to the United States.

About 7 percent of adults in Europe reported frequent loneliness in the past week—that is, feeling lonely "all or almost all the time" or "most of the time." The percentage is higher in Hungary, the Czech Republic, Italy, Poland, France, and Greece, and it's lower in the Netherlands, Denmark, Finland, Germany, Ireland, and Sweden.[a]

The United Kingdom has similar rates of loneliness compared to the United States, with 23 percent of adults reporting that they always or often feel lonely.[b] Among European countries, its rate of loneliness is somewhere in the middle of the pack.

One major difference between Europe and the United States is that self-reported loneliness had not increased in Europe since the 2010s.[c]

Loneliness is spread unevenly in most countries. Almost universally, it hits those who are of low socioeconomic status or poor health harder.[d] Other aspects of life that might shed light on loneliness include culture, economic opportunity, marriage ages and rates, even commute times and living arrangements. These are all very hard to untangle. It does seem that the secondary sources of loneliness—that is, the exact form that disappointment in relationships takes—are different in different cultures.[e] This may well be because different behaviors signal intimacy, or different expectations let people in for emotional pain.

Loneliness among older adults gets a good deal of attention abroad as well as in the United States—and for good reason. The death rate in this population is higher, and the link between loneliness, social isolation, and death is more clear and more urgent. Also, people are on average older than they used to be because of dramatically increased life expectancy around the world, a pattern going back many decades.[f]

The patterns of loneliness and age in different countries vary (see fig. 1.1). In the United States and New Zealand, there is a pattern of decreasing loneliness until later old age, when there is an uptick.[g] In Russia and Spain, the older people are, the likelier they are to be lonely. In the United Kingdom and Sweden, young adults are lonelier than middle-aged adults and less lonely than older adults. In Denmark, old and young adults are about equally lonely, and middle-aged adults are less lonely.[h]

Connected Generation Study

Barna and World Vision International looked into the lives of eighteen- to thirty-five-year-olds in countries around the world in the Connected Generation project.[i] Of a huge sample of over fifteen thousand young people responding to a survey translated into nine languages, Barna asked if they often felt "lonely and isolated."

Differences fell along the usual lines: increasing age, being married, more reliable employment, and emotional security all predict less loneliness, as they do across generations in the United States. About a quarter of young adults in this international sample said they often feel lonely and isolated from others.

Young people in the United States were among the loneliest of the twenty-five countries surveyed in the study (see fig. 1.2). One-third (34%) of young American adults said they often felt lonely and isolated from others, a very similar proportion to the United Kingdom (31%), Australia (34%), and New Zealand (31%), and somewhat higher than Canada (29%), Chile (28%), South Africa (26%), and Malaysia (25%).

Figure 1.1

Proportion of Adults Who Feel Lonely Frequently

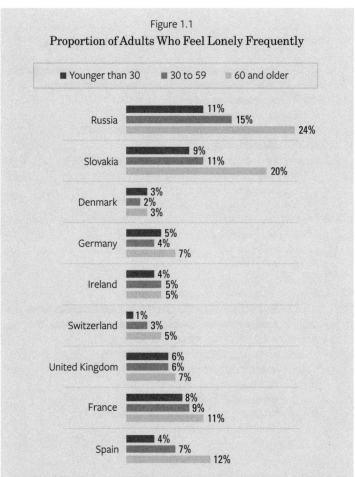

Adapted from Keming Yang and Christina Victor, "Age and Loneliness in 25 European Nations," *Ageing and Society* 31, no. 8 (2011): 1376, https://doi.org/10.1017/S0144686X1000139X.

While many researchers have looked for patterns in loneliness among people in different countries, the reasons for rates of loneliness are elusive. In this data, however, there is an intriguing pattern: the more advanced a country in this study is on the UN's Human Development Index, the lonelier its young people say they are. The

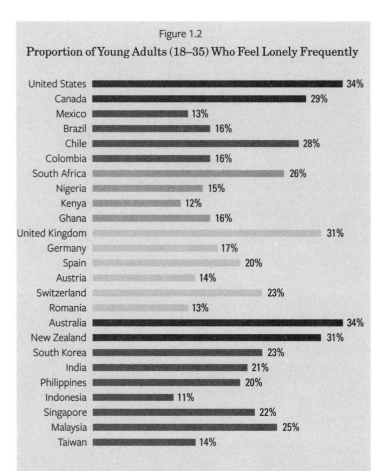

Figure 1.2

Proportion of Young Adults (18–35) Who Feel Lonely Frequently

United States	34%
Canada	29%
Mexico	13%
Brazil	16%
Chile	28%
Colombia	16%
South Africa	26%
Nigeria	15%
Kenya	12%
Ghana	16%
United Kingdom	31%
Germany	17%
Spain	20%
Austria	14%
Switzerland	23%
Romania	13%
Australia	34%
New Zealand	31%
South Korea	23%
India	21%
Philippines	20%
Indonesia	11%
Singapore	22%
Malaysia	25%
Taiwan	14%

Human Development Index measures a set of factors, including life expectancy, education, and per capita income. While the benefits of a long life, literacy, and even high income are clear, something mixed in with the lifestyle of countries high in these factors is also producing lonely young adults.

Religious practice also plays a role (see fig. 1.3). In this group of young adults, those who feel closest to their religion feel the least lonely. Only 16 percent of practicing Christians and 15 percent of those practicing another religion say they often feel isolated and

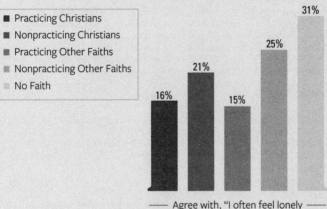

Figure 1.3

Young Adults in Various Countries Who Feel Lonely Frequently
Percentages by Religious Affiliation

- ■ Practicing Christians
- ■ Nonpracticing Christians
- ■ Practicing Other Faiths
- ■ Nonpracticing Other Faiths
- ■ No Faith

16% 21% 15% 25% 31%

—— Agree with, "I often feel lonely ——
and isolated from others."

lonely, about two-thirds the rate of the total (23%). Twenty-one percent of nonpracticing Christians say the same, about the same rate as young people who are nonpracticing members of a non-Christian faith (in this sample, most of those were Muslim, Buddhist, Hindu, or practitioners of indigenous religions). The nones—those without a faith—had the highest proportion of lonely people, at 31 percent.

Even without very high rates of loneliness, some countries are taking action at a national level. These include initiatives like the appointment of a loneliness minister in the United Kingdom and Denmark's Princess Mary attending a communal meal organized by members of the anti-loneliness campaign Denmark Eats Together. These are great ideas, I think, reinforcing a country's desire to take care of everyone.

I hope the loneliness epidemic in the United States will inspire a response on a similar (or greater) scale and in a way that suits our culture, where voluntary organizations like churches have often taken a lead. Addressing loneliness in the whole population—not just older adults—will play a big role in the success of any anti-loneliness initiative.

a. Béatrice d'Hombres, Sylke Schnepf, Martina Barjaková, and Francisco Teixeira Mendonça, "Loneliness—an Unequally Shared Burden in Europe," EU Science Hub, 2018, 1, https://ec.europa.eu/jrc/sites/jrcsh/files/fairness_pb2018_loneliness_jrc_i1.pdf.

b. Bianca DiJulio, Liz Hamel, Cailey Muñana, and Mollyann Brodie, "Loneliness and Social Isolation in the United States, the United Kingdom, and Japan: An International Survey," Kaiser Family Foundation, August 30, 2018, 3, https://www.kff.org/other/report/loneliness-and-social-isolation-in-the-united-states-the-united-kingdom-and-japan-an-international-survey/.

c. D'Hombres et al., "Loneliness," 2.

d. DiJulio et al., "Loneliness and Social Isolation," 4–5.

e. DiJulio et al., "Loneliness and Social Isolation," 19.

f. "Population Ages 65 and above (% of Total Population)," World Bank, 2019, https://data.worldbank.org/indicator/SP.POP.65UP.TO.ZS.

g. Ministry of Social Development, "Loneliness," in *The Social Report 2016—Te Pūrongo Oranga Tangata* (Wellington: Ministry of Social Development, 2016), https://socialreport.msd.govt.nz/social-connectedness/loneliness.html.

h. Keming Yang and Christina Victor, "Age and Loneliness in 25 European Nations," *Ageing and Society* 31, no. 8 (2011): 1376, https://doi.org/10.1017/S0144686X1000139X.

i. Barna Group, *The Connected Generation: How Christian Leaders around the World Can Strengthen Faith and Well-Being among 18–35-Year-Olds* (Ventura, CA: Barna Group, 2019), 47, https://theconnectedgeneration.com/.

2

WHAT LONELINESS IS

A Definition of Terms

Jesus "often withdrew to lonely places and prayed" (Luke 5:16). In one of his poems, Wordsworth "wandered lonely as a cloud."[1] Similarly, the Backstreet Boys beseeched all their fans to "show me the meaning of being lonely."[2] I don't know if they have their answer yet, but it's understandable that they'd be confused, given how many meanings *lonely* has.

Why does *lonely* have such a wide range of meanings? The short answer is that its meaning has changed over time. I'll show how and then define the specific use that it has taken on today.

Defining Loneliness

When *lonely* originally appeared in English literature, it meant solitude.

The Online Etymology Dictionary says that the word *lonely* made its first known written appearance in English in about 1600 and that *loneliness* appeared before that in a 1580 document.[3] Both words had to do more with who someone was physically with—in solitude or the wilderness—than with an emotional state. The King James Bible was completed a few years later and didn't include either variation of the word. Shakespeare used *lonely* or *loneliness* only a few times throughout his works.

English speakers still had a way to talk about the feeling we call loneliness today. At that time, if you wanted to express that you were feeling dejected because you lacked fellowship, you might have said you were *loneful*, a term that popped up in the 1560s, or *lonesome*, which was used from the 1640s on.

By the early 1800s, you could have used *lonely* and *loneliness* to describe that same ache. The use of *lonely* peaked in American literature not long after that, in the mid-1800s. While

Important Terms (Barna Group)

Gen Z: Born between 2003 and 2015

Millennials: Born between 1984 and 2002

Gen X: Born between 1965 and 1983

Boomers: Born between 1946 and 1964

Elders: Born 1945 or earlier

Born-again Christians: Those who have made a personal commitment to Jesus Christ that is still important in their lives today and who believe that when they die they will go to heaven because they have confessed their sins and accepted Jesus Christ as their Savior

Practicing Christians: Those who attend a religious service at least once a month, who say their faith is very important in their lives and who self-identify as Christians

Nonpracticing Christians: Those who self-identify as Christians but do not qualify as practicing Christians because of attending church infrequently or not agreeing strongly that their faith is very important in their lives or both

Non-Christians: Those who do not self-identify as Christians

it's on the rise again, it hasn't yet hit the same proportion of words in books as in the Civil War era.

While we still encounter those older versions of *lonely* and *loneliness* meaning solitude, today they are now the default terms for disappointment over companionship. I'll delve into what is and isn't true about that later. For now, keep in mind that solitude in this book may have little to do with someone's loneliness.

Here, as in the academic research, loneliness is *the distress someone feels when their social connections don't meet their need for emotional intimacy*. So, it's lack. It's disappointment. It's something we are conscious of, even when we don't call it loneliness. Loneliness is a thirst that drives us to seek companionship—or, perhaps better, fellowship. Without fellowship, we go on needing others and seeking relief for that need.

Marilynne Robinson's books all contain themes of loneliness and the difficulty of intimacy. In *Lila*, the main character, a woman who has often been homeless, experiences loneliness this way: "She had told herself more than once not to call it loneliness, since it wasn't any different from one year to the next, it was just how her body felt, like hungry or tired, except it was always there, always the same."[4]

Loneliness, like other needs, nags. It's not a state that feels right to us, even when it's chronic. In that sense, loneliness, like pain, is a gift. It drives us to something better and healthier, a life more like the one God made us for.

Rates of Loneliness

Imagine you wake up one morning with a third of your body aching, everything from your neck to your waist. And in that area a small part of you—one of your lungs—is in outright pain. You've had a cold and a cough for a couple weeks and noticed a tightness in your chest, but you'd been hoping until now that it would just go away. Now you know for sure you can't ignore it; it's off to the nearest urgent care center.

Now, imagine that description isn't you catching a suspected case of pneumonia but rather America experiencing loneliness.

The country is sick with respect to people's ability to have close, trusting relationships—one of the most important parts of our humanity. Where we need and look for intimacy and friendship, too many of us are disappointed. Like our ability to breathe, our ability to find fellowship affects everything else we do. With at least a third of the country suffering, it's no wonder loneliness is getting a lot of attention these days. In fact, we're having an epidemic of loneliness.

America isn't a body the way the church is, but it is still a society in which we share the consequences of epidemics. When part of our society is hurting, it affects us in many ways; our culture, the feeling we get from our neighborhoods, and our ability to take care of problems together all suffer.

One-third (33%) of US adults felt lonely at least every day in the winter of 2020, and a majority had felt lonely in the past week (see fig. 2.1). That means half of Americans are suffering

Figure 2.1

US Adults' Frequency of Loneliness in Winter 2020

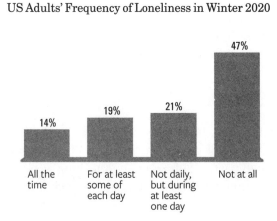

from loneliness. About one in seven (14%) Americans indicated they felt lonely all the time. That's only slightly rarer than owning both a cat and a dog.[5] One in five (19%) said they felt lonely for at least some of each day. Another fifth (21%) said they had felt lonely not daily but during at least one day of the past week.

These numbers give us a snapshot of loneliness. What they don't reveal is for whom loneliness is a long-term, chronic condition. The chronic version of loneliness is more damaging. One study found that between 15 and 30 percent of Americans have chronic loneliness.[6] That is, between one in seven and one in three people have been lonely for a long, long time.

Those whose loneliness is constant and chronic have likely experienced how loneliness can chip away at health and quality of life.

Severity of Loneliness

And how does loneliness feel? Not usually that bad.

In the winter of 2020, about a fifth (21%) of US adults said loneliness is always bad, and two-fifths (40%) said loneliness is never good. It might not seem like it, but there is wiggle room between "always bad" and "never good." That includes the ideas of neutrality and exceptions to "always" and "never." So we're more inclined to think loneliness can range from bad to neutral, but many Americans also see ways that loneliness can be good.

None of this is to say that Americans look forward to loneliness. As of the winter of 2020, more than a quarter (28%) of US adults say loneliness is always unpleasant. Over half (55%) say it is sometimes unpleasant. Eighteen percent say it is never unpleasant. (I suspect they are thinking of solitude rather than loneliness—more about that below.)

Still, these perceptions of loneliness sound more like our opinions on running a 5k than on confronting an epidemic.

Figure 2.2
Lonely US Adults' Pain of Loneliness in Winter 2020:
"How Painful Would You Say Your Feelings of Loneliness Were?"

| 12% | 19% | 25% | 22% | 14% | 6% | 3% |

Barely noticeable   Intense   Unbearable

Unpleasant though it may be, loneliness isn't always miserable, even when you're experiencing it.

Most people who feel lonely at least weekly say that it's intense but not excruciating. On a seven-point pain scale of "barely noticeable" to "unbearable," with "intense" as the middle option, most lonely Americans put their pain at about a point easier than "intense" (see fig. 2.2). About a third (31%) of lonely Americans say their loneliness is barely noticeable or a degree more intense. Three in five (61%) lonely Americans say their pain of loneliness is within a point of "intense."

That's where the good news ends.

About one in ten lonely Americans are suffering deeply, saying their loneliness is unbearable or one point easier.

To give a sense of how common this is, think about how many teachers, librarians, or professors you know or know of—probably quite a few. Their lives likely touch yours at many points. The number of people experiencing nearly unbearable loneliness (nearly ten million, extrapolated from the 209 million adults in the United States) is about the same as the number of Americans employed as educators.[7]

Loneliness as an Epidemic

The idea that a feeling—loneliness—can be an epidemic strikes many as strange. *Epidemic* is usually reserved for an unexpected increase in the rate of disease caused by bacteria or viruses, the sort of thing that can be solved with quarantines or vaccines or sewerage.

It is time, however, to stop thinking of health as having to do only with germs and pills. We understand very little of how our bodies interact with our food and our environment, let alone how our bodies interact with our thoughts, beliefs, and feelings. Still, we know for sure there are profound connections.

Former US surgeon general Vivek Murthy, author of *Together: The Healing Power of Human Connection in a Sometimes Lonely World*, said in 2017 that loneliness was an epidemic; its growth has accelerated and become a public problem.[8] The United States is, in fact, undergoing multiple mysterious epidemics, according to the surgeons general: the opioid epidemic, the obesity epidemic, the HIV/AIDS epidemic, the vaping epidemic, the suicide epidemic. All of this in addition to the COVID-19 pandemic. (A pandemic is an epidemic around the world.)

According to the *Washington Post*, loneliness rates have doubled since the 1980s.[9] Cigna found that in 2019, 61 percent of Americans were lonely, a seven-percentage-point rise from the survey a year before. That may not sound like much, but it's still fifteen million more lonely people. And if loneliness increased at that rate every two years, every adult would be lonely by 2025. (Note that each year, 7 percent is more people than the year before, since the United States is growing.)

But that isn't likely to happen; epidemics don't tend to increase at the same rate. In fact, they tend to increase exponentially at first. That is, instead of each person spreading the trouble to one other person, each person spreads it to several. That's how a wedding with one or two sick people on August 9, 2020, ended up spreading COVID-19 to 177 people just a little more than a month later.[10] Loneliness, too, spreads person to person.

How Loneliness Spreads

We know how loneliness spreads because of a remarkable study on heart disease called the Framingham Heart Study. Researchers' eyes pop when they see the participation rate—an unheard-of majority of the town at the beginning of the study. Such a high proportion of people answering health and lifestyle questions for so long (three generations!) means that researchers can trace all sorts of social and physical phenomena.

One of these is loneliness. Every few years, Framingham residents answered a few questions about loneliness. But then the authors of an article titled "Alone in the Crowd" took it a step further.[11]

In case participants moved or couldn't be reached for the next round of interviews, the Framingham researchers had asked them to name "relatives, friends, neighbors, co-workers . . . who might be in a position to know where the [participants] would be in two to four years."[12] With a majority of the community participating, those relationships could be both cross-referenced and traced over time.

The result was data on people's experience of loneliness with some incredible information on their social networks. It was a picture of one-sided friendships and of mutual friendships; of people who were physically close throughout the day; of kin relationships and of relationships people chose and nurtured. And the map of the relationships looked like a tangled piece of a seaweed like red algae. Some of its blades are full of lonely people, and others are not. Where the blades meet the stem, there are few lonely people.

The researchers found that loneliness, like so many other things, spreads person to person. Someone is 52 percent more likely to be lonely if they're directly connected to another lonely person.[13] Loneliness spreads like contagion.

But the contagion of loneliness doesn't start just anywhere. It starts with the people on the edges. In the nodes of the social network are people with strong mutual ties. They list contacts and are listed as contacts by the same people, forming dense tangles where people are mutually important to each other and the mutual relationships are thick.

On the lonely blades of Framingham's social network, people may list fewer contacts, or those contacts may not list them, indicating a relationship that is lopsided and barely mutual. Those people tend to say they are lonelier.

As one lonely person's loneliness spreads to another, the edges of the community crumble. Communities that are plagued by loneliness are like icebergs with chunks falling off the edges. The connections that bind them are threatened as more and more people become lonely.[14]

Loneliness and the Body

There's worse news about loneliness than that it is often emotionally painful: loneliness kills.

Murthy mentions in interview after interview statistics showing that loneliness shortens a person's life about as much as smoking fifteen cigarettes a day. He points out that that's more than the impact of obesity on the length of our lives.[15] Even when age, sex, chronic diseases, alcohol use, smoking, self-rated health, and physical limitations are accounted for, loneliness still predicts earlier death.[16]

Death is likely the scariest of loneliness's physical effects, but there are many more. Heart disease is one of the main medical problems loneliness contributes to. In fact, the effect of loneliness is so strong on heart disease that it amounts to a dose-response relationship: the more loneliness over the course of a person's life, the more heart damage. Other problems that have to do with heart disease also accompany loneliness: obesity and raised blood pressure.[17] One study found that even though depression often accompanies coronary heart disease, loneliness had an additional effect in a group of women, making them even more vulnerable.[18]

And when you've already had heart trouble, loneliness will keep you down; lonely heart failure patients were four times as likely as not-lonely heart failure patients to die.[19]

Inflammatory responses are part of the body's complicated way of dealing with perceived threats. You're having an inflammatory response if you start a fever or develop a hot, swollen spot or if you sniffle and sneeze. Often our bodies are fighting off the attacks of bacteria or viruses when we have an inflammatory response—but not always. Autoimmune diseases like arthritis are inflammatory responses against fake dangers; they are our bodies attacking themselves. A damaged inflammatory response is one of the symptoms of loneliness.[20]

When our bodies are fighting real enemies, we need strong, functional immune systems. But when we are lonely, we have fewer effective monocytes, infection-fighting white blood cells, in our systems.[21] Our ability to fight off diseases suffers.[22]

Another dreaded symptom, dementia, often accompanies loneliness in old age. Older people who feel lonely are more than twice as likely as others to develop Alzheimer's disease.[23] Loneliness worsens Alzheimer's over and above the harm of another common problem: depression.[24] Lonely older people are far more likely to have trouble with elements of dementia, even if they don't have Alzheimer's. In general, loneliness contributes to cognitive decline.[25] Such people may seem less with-it as they age. In a study of loneliness in older Americans, lonelier people became senile at a higher rate over several years. They lost much more of their ability and quickness to understand and learn and struggled with memory.[26]

Lots of research shows that loneliness leads to stress and that good-enough relationships prevent it.[27] Most emotional anguish has physical effects. Under forms of stress, like loneliness, our bodies produce hormones (cortisol and norepinephrine in particular)[28] to be ready for a fight-or-flight response. When we live with them constantly, they start to damage us. We get sick more frequently and recover more slowly.

Sleep is not only dear to my heart; it's also increasingly known to be a factor in physical and mental health. Most of us think of people as needing eight hours of sleep a night, but that's the minimum for teenagers and the midpoint for adults. A third of US adults get less than the minimum (seven hours) of sleep a night, with low-income Americans hit hardest; among teenagers, more than two-thirds don't get enough sleep.[29] Lack of sleep can hurt our ability to process our emotions and interactions. Short nights are for emergencies and newborns, not for watching movies or thinking we can put in a bit more work. But even when lonely people are pretty good about going to bed, their sleep is damaged.

In one experiment about loneliness, a sleep lab tracked sixty-four people, half men, half women.[30] A third were very lonely, a third were somewhat lonely, and a third weren't lonely, but the experimenters didn't know who was in which group. From what the experimenters knew, they all had about the same chance of sleeping well. Night came, and the technology kicked in. Sensors tracked the participants' eyes under their eyelids and their head movements. They determined how long after trying to sleep each person became still. They tracked when people thrashed and how much they woke up when they moved in their sleep.

The lonely people were restless sleepers. They moved more, waking up more often, even if they didn't remember it, and spending more time awake. That was both in the sleep lab and afterward, at home.

Loneliness is also connected to depression and suicide.[31] Those connections have not been studied extensively, unfortunately. All forms of mental illness seem to bring loneliness along with their other symptoms, and depression is one of these.

Suicidal ideation, which doesn't always accompany loneliness, nevertheless shares with depression and loneliness a distorted view of one's belonging and relationships. With suicide being one of the top killers in America and depression on the rise, it's time we learned whether new approaches to loneliness could save people from mental illness, either its onset or its recurrence.

Loneliness also has an economic cost in lost productivity, as well as sick days and earlier deaths. It takes a toll on problem-solving and saps our memories and decision-making abilities.[32]

In summary, chronic loneliness can be deadly, but it also makes us less healthy, less able to think, and more physically uncomfortable. There's a strong case to be made that governments, employers, and insurance companies should worry about increases in loneliness, if only for their own bottom line. Yet any sort of fix will take something that governments, employers, and insurance companies are not good at engineering: quality relationships.

Importance of Relationships

Loneliness is about relationships. And what aspect of humanity is more important than relationships? While people don't start friendships with every person they meet, they do form social bonds with "remarkable ease."[33] And yet we have to exert a lot of effort and extend a lot of grace to keep them going. The need to belong in networks of relationships seems to counteract other human tendencies, like competitiveness and jealousy, that drive people apart.[34]

In the twentieth century, psychologists tended to assume that humans were driven by our ugliest desires or by loyalty to kin. But when tested, it turns out that our actions are more often explained by our need to belong. For example, some researchers thought that people became anxious and then jealous because they anticipated an insult. But instead, they found anxiety was because of the anticipated loss of that relationship.[35] Relationships are precious to us—to every one of us.

We know about God through a relationship. Even if we worshiped a cold, unresponsive God, we would still be attempting a relationship with him. We don't, of course, worship a cold, unresponsive God. We worship a warm, loving God who finds it intolerable when he can't gather recalcitrant people under his wings like a mother hen. We worship a God who over and over describes the great worth of each one of us to himself and his angels. When we are saved, he rejoices over us. When we start walking toward him, he runs toward us. When we grieve, he grieves with us.

Loneliness is not a problem that can be solved by anything short of love.

Two Kinds of Loneliness

Some researchers have tried to split loneliness into components, with little success.

One useful division remains: some loneliness is because we want company—almost any buddy will do—and some loneliness is because we lack a specific person in a special relationship, as when we grieve a spouse. (These are, unhelpfully, referred to as "social" and "emotional" loneliness, respectively.)

The loneliness that has to do with the amount of social interaction varies widely by person. Extroverts are known for needing more buddy time and often more buddies. A buddy may not have met your spouse, but he or she probably has seen what you pack for lunch and probably feels close enough to tease you. Buddies seek each other out and enjoy each other's company. Not to minimize friendships or friends, but buddy relationships seem to be interchangeable. That is, if one of your friends can't hang out, you can hang out with someone else and be none the lonelier.

Extroverts seem to need more buddies to not feel lonely, but for everyone there are diminishing returns.[36] Your first few buddies help a lot with loneliness, but as you add more and more buddies, they matter less to loneliness.

Loneliness experts Roy Baumeister and Mark Leary found that "generally, loneliness seems to be a matter more of a lack of intimate connections than of a lack of social contact."[37] In other words, when people are deeply lonely, they usually need intimacy, not company.

Some friendships go beyond buddy-hood in intimacy. I don't mean physical intimacy alone, and I certainly don't mean sexual intimacy. Intimate friends are confidants; they are people who have heard you fart or know how you feel not only about your spouse's loud chewing but also about the way your mother talks to your father or what it means when you laugh a certain way. They're people whom you can depend on emotionally.

In addition to that closeness and trust, there's probably mutual love.

Then there are some relationships that are so special that no one can switch in or out without grief and a period to let it fade. Spouses are the most relevant to loneliness in this category, since marriage makes a bigger difference in loneliness than most other relationships. We can have these close and all-but-irreplaceable relationships with parents, children, siblings, and best friends too.

Not Quite Loneliness

It's worth clarifying what loneliness is not. Loneliness can thrive even in situations we often think of as warding off loneliness, such as being in crowds or with loved ones. It may help, then, to have a few more definitions, specifically about social isolation and solitude—both often confused with loneliness.

For example, one of the loneliest situations I can think of is to be the spouse of a patient in the hospital. Is the loneliest part holding a little baggie with a wedding ring? Or is it sitting alone in the waiting room with other families speaking in hushed voices? Is it realizing that your spouse might be different from this point on? Notice that in that scenario, you're not by yourself. You're with a loved one. You're not in private, really. You're receiving help, as is your loved one. But you might be terribly lonely all the same.

Social Isolation

Social isolation is when a person doesn't have much contact with others. Unlike loneliness, which is subjective, social isolation is objective. To put it bluntly, people are resources and give resources to each other. We deliver news, mail, groceries, and more. We teach each other our culture (usually indirectly) and respond to each other's behavior. We help each other when we need it. We advise each other to see doctors about lumps.

Socially isolated people may be found in restaurants, on buses, even in workplaces. But nobody checks up on them. They neither know nor are known deeply by others.

Imagine someone who didn't receive any human help or interaction. They could have once been close to others, or not. But in the life of a completely isolated person, there would be no hugs, no talking to neighbors over the fence, no Zoom meetings outside of work, no Thanksgiving dinners, no bringing anyone coffee in the morning, no laughing with someone else, no concerned woman putting a hand on their forehead to test for fever.

People with a dearth of social interaction tend to lose track of many important things. In fact, they are more likely to die. For example, someone living alone might be more likely to suffer from heat stroke because she doesn't have someone who comes to check in on her during hot summer days.[38] Married men live longer for a tangle of reasons, but very clearly because something about having a wife helps them avoid death.[39]

Social isolation is also bad for the health of just about every social animal we study. One study has collected these results: social isolation makes fruit flies die earlier; mice develop type 2 diabetes; rats stop enjoying some benefits of exercise. It damages pigs' immune responses, exaggerates the natural rise in squirrel monkeys' stress hormones in the morning, and "profoundly disrupts psychosexual development in rhesus monkeys."[40] In people, it's almost unheard-of to be both very happy and very socially isolated.[41]

As you might imagine, there is overlap between loneliness and social isolation, but the connection isn't overwhelmingly strong. In a study of older Americans, loneliness predicted only about a fifth of social isolation.[42] That's about as loose a connection as there is between height and IQ[43]—not a good bet in a world that produced shorties like James Madison and Mahatma Gandhi. Likewise, if you know someone is lonely, you shouldn't assume they are socially isolated.

Nevertheless, researchers and others have raised the question: Is loneliness really a separate problem from social isolation?

The clear answer is yes: they are separate problems leading to health problems and a raised risk of early death.[44] The degree of risk from loneliness and social isolation is similar.

By all means, we should address social isolation. But leaders and others with kind intentions shouldn't confuse bringing resources to isolated people with addressing loneliness.

Solitude

Solitude is a second factor to keep in mind when we talk about loneliness. Solitude is simply being alone. People can't be in solitude on the bus or in line at a restaurant; they are not alone. But people with busy lives and close relationships can be in solitude from time to time.

Solitude can be delicious. A long walk in the woods or a day at home with a good book and no one else around may sound lovely to many, particularly people who have hidden in the bathroom to try to get some time alone.

In her collection of essays *When I Was a Child I Read Books*, Marilynne Robinson writes,

> I remember when I was a child at Coolin or Sagle or Talache, walking into the woods by myself and feeling the solitude around me build like electricity and pass through my body with a jolt that made my hair prickle. I remember kneeling by a creek that spilled and pooled among rocks and fallen trees with the unspeakably tender growth of small trees already sprouting from their backs, and thinking, there is only one thing wrong here, which is my own presence, and that is the slightest imaginable intrusion—feeling that my solitude, my loneliness, made me almost acceptable in so sacred a place.[45]

People need solitude. A reasonable amount of solitude helps us process. It seems to increase our ability to reach our potential, to self-regulate, and to put our experiences in context. It increases creativity.[46]

People who are lonely may or may not be in solitude, and people in solitude may or may not be lonely. People in solitude for extended periods of time are socially isolated, but people in solitude intermittently will probably find it feels good.

Linford Detweiler of Over the Rhine said, "When Karin and I moved out of the city to a small hideaway farm, it was both a healthy move for us and a challenging one. I slowly came to make a distinction between solitude, which was healthy and welcome (a necessary discipline for writers), and isolation, which felt depleting or like something was missing. So as a writer, I've tried to value and make room for solitude, but I've been wary of being too isolated—cut off from people who inspire me, know me, hear me."[47]

Even the pandemic has helped with sorting out the feelings and tensions of being more alone, Detweiler says. "For the most part, the pandemic slowing things down for us has felt like a good thing on a personal level. We didn't realize how grateful we would be to have permission to hold still for a while. In retrospect, we really did need a break from the road. Of course, there have been financial challenges, and we miss performing, but the deep solitude has been mostly healing for us. We've been able to find plenty of silver linings."[48]

For each of the feelings we experience because of our involvement with others, there is a time. A time to be alone. A time to be in a crowd. A time for privacy. A time for openness. A time to call your mother. A time to refrain from calling your mother. A time to Zoom. A time to walk in the woods by yourself. A time to talk to yourself. A time to be quiet because your colleague is listening to you talk to yourself.

We need the pressures and blessings of those around us. Most of us seem to accept this, expecting and even embracing the ebb and flow of loneliness and social contact. Loneliness is manageable for most of us. Still, chronic and painful loneliness are damaging our society as well as many individuals in it. We are suffering in several dimensions of our humanity.

After periods of loneliness and even social isolation, we need to be re-enveloped in satisfying and reliable relationships. And we can help make that happen for each other, especially if we better understand who is suffering.

Part 2

WHEN LONELINESS DEFIES STEREOTYPES

When it comes to lonely people, we often think of stereotypes such as an elderly spinster whiling away the hours with knitting or a basement-dwelling dweeb who never gets the girl.

And, of course, there's the Beatles' earworm "Eleanor Rigby," which paints a picture of two lives. One is a spinster who "lives in a dream" and "waits at the window," and when she dies, nobody comes to her funeral. The other is a priest who prepares for a no-show congregation and whose work is ineffective.

We also stereotype the never-lonely: a happy couple with straight-A children, a social media queen, a college student overscheduled for parties. This could also be one of those people who is on every committee and always seems to be going from one meeting or coffee with a friend to another.

There is some truth to these profiles, but not a lot. Not everyone you or I pity is lonely; not every subject of jealousy feels belonging.

Fighting loneliness means checking up on our intuitions about who is lonely. Leaders protect against loneliness by challenging their stereotypes. Many common ideas about who is lonesome are backward. Fortunately, there is a good deal of research that can clear all of this up. In the following chapters, I address the myths, the truth in the myths, and the clearest paths to help the lonely.

3

AGE

MYTH: Older adults are the loneliest.

One afternoon in the summer of 2020, when DC's COVID-19 regulations were loose enough that we could go outside as much as we wanted, my baby wouldn't take a nap. I strapped him into a carrier and started walking through my neighborhood. A few blocks from home, I came across two people standing about ten feet apart on a wide sidewalk: a gray-haired woman in a mask and a man with his mask below his chin.

The man was talking. The woman was giving off polite but recognizable signals that she would like to exit the conversation. As she edged away, the man turned his attention to me like a magnet snapping to the closest metal.

When he judged the other woman to be out of hearing distance, he told me that he always tried to talk to old ladies, since they must be very lonely. He went on to regale me with his professional accomplishments. I slapped at mosquitoes and nodded. My baby fell asleep at last. It started to rain. I forget how the conversation ended—I have no gift for timely interruption—but I walked away thinking, *I think that poor lady and I know we weren't the lonely ones*.

Our whole society has a similar attitude to that man's: we are trying so hard to draw attention to the loneliness of older adults that we've failed to notice that they aren't the lonely ones.

Generation Makes a Difference in Loneliness

People's ages have a huge effect on whether they say they experience loneliness and on how painful it is. It may be hard for younger people to see the joys of being over sixty-five, but there is plenty of evidence that joy may be more accessible in your sixties than in your twenties.

US generations follow a clear pattern in how frequently they say they are lonely: the oldest are the least lonely, and each

Figure 3.1
Frequency of US Adults' Loneliness in Winter 2020 by Generation

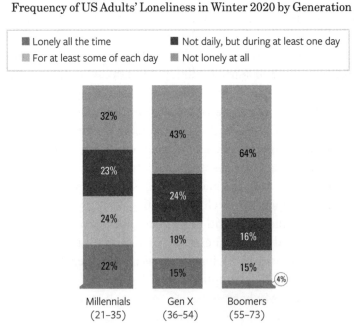

subsequent generation is lonelier (see fig. 3.1). Elders are least likely to say they are lonely, followed by Boomers, Gen X, Millennials, and Gen Z.

In the winter of 2020, 64 percent of Boomers said they had not felt lonely in the past week. Forty-three percent of Gen X said so, along with 32 percent of Millennials.

Sixteen percent of Boomers, 24 percent of Gen X, and a similar proportion of younger adults said they had felt lonely not daily but during at least one day of the past week. The most intense frequency of loneliness was greatest in the youngest generations.

Another important dimension of loneliness, in addition to frequency, is severity. US adults who felt lonely in the past week also showed differences in the pain of their loneliness according to their generation (see fig. 3.2).

Among the subgroup of those who were lonely during the winter of 2020, the pattern is that the older lonely Americans are, the less likely they are to say they suffer much from their loneliness—another strike against the stereotype of age bringing loneliness.

Figure 3.2

Pain of US Adults' Loneliness in Winter 2020 by Generation

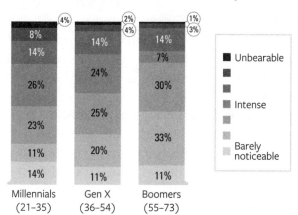

The pattern of falling loneliness and falling pain of loneliness doesn't hold all the way through the Elders generation, or those who are seventy-four or older. There are a couple reasons for that.

First, there is a small sample size. That is, of the people who took this survey, the group of Elders is relatively small, and it's shrinking as this generation passes away. It's hard to be sure that respondents to this survey represent the whole group of their generation without surveying many more people. (This is why I seldom cite specific percentages for this group.) So researchers don't put a lot of weight on how perfectly they fit into the pattern. Second, there are reasons to think that this uptick in loneliness is genuine and not just a fluke: as people go well past their retirement years, their lives start to change in significant ways.

Stigma and Loneliness

People may have multiple reasons for saying they're not lonely. One significant reason is that they think it's the "wrong" answer.

I wondered if older Americans stigmatized loneliness and were therefore reluctant to admit to it. But the data shows that in some ways young Americans have a harsher view of loneliness than their elders do. Millennials were more likely than Gen X or Boomers to say loneliness was always embarrassing. And, perhaps surprisingly, many older adults said loneliness is never embarrassing. Two-thirds (68%) of Boomers said loneliness is never embarrassing, compared to 54 percent of Gen X and 37 percent of Millennials. There weren't notable generational differences in the proportions who said loneliness is always or never bad, but differences reappeared in the proportions who said loneliness is never good—this time flipped. Between a quarter and a third of Americans under fifty-five said loneliness is never good, but at least half of older generations said it is never good.

But there was a bigger surprise: young people were least likely to say loneliness is never sinful. Just over half (57%) of Millennials said loneliness is never sinful. For older generations, this rose to represent the overwhelming majority view. Seventy percent of Gen X and 87 percent of Boomers said loneliness is never sinful.

Calling loneliness sinful may reflect some spurious answers or a flippant attitude toward sin on the part of younger Americans. But it may also give us an idea that young adults expect censure and rejection over their loneliness.

Older adults' attitudes toward loneliness don't indicate that they would avoid admitting to loneliness, even if they are not eager to embrace it. Rather, the stigma seems strongest among the young.

Young, Scrappy, and Lonely

Given that older Americans have bucked the stereotype of loneliness, how do we explain the loneliness of young Americans? One explanation sums it up: transitions.

A study of loneliness across the life span indicates that people seem to accumulate loneliness, particularly at "developmental occasions" like adolescence.[1] And as we hit different developmental phases, our social needs change. We need different kinds of relationships to avoid loneliness.

One study found that "children move from simply wanting to be physically close to others to wanting close friendships that are characterized by validation, understanding, self-disclosure, and empathy."[2] In other words, while we might have felt satisfied with other kids who played jump rope or soccer with us in our early school years, soon enough we want those friends to not just do things with us; we want them to tell us secrets and keep ours. We want them to wear the other half of a best friends heart necklace. We want them around when something goes wrong in our families.

As they grow through elementary school years, children become increasingly aware of where they stand in the pecking order. If they feel rejected by their peers—a key source of loneliness at this stage—they really suffer over it. Adolescents need a close friend but still feel lonely if they feel unliked by their peers.

In early adulthood—the phase we're most concerned with here—romantic relationships become more important to loneliness. They remain in a key role throughout adulthood, shifting later on to marital status instead of just relationship status.

Transitions aren't what they used to be, nor are the marks of adulthood. Young adults' key relationships are timed and circumscribed differently now than they were when Boomers and Gen X were young. It would take—and has taken—books to go into all the dynamics of delayed marriage and childbearing in the United States. I want to focus on a few transitions and changes in relationship satisfaction.

The most important marker of adulthood to today's young adults comes with a tassel: completed education. Three in five young adults (62%) rank this as very important to adulthood. Increasingly, this means a four-year degree, but it may also mean a high school diploma.

After completed education, young adults believe adulthood comes with a few markers of economic independence: full-time employment (52% say it's very important), becoming financially capable of supporting a family (50%), and becoming financially independent from parents (43%) round out the top four.[3]

Young adults believe they should have achieved these adult markers by their early twenties, but in fact they are unlikely to hit those goals in that time range. By age twenty-two, only 52 percent have completed their education, whether a high school diploma, a four-year degree, another goal, or by quitting postsecondary education. Just over a third of young adults have a full-time job by the time they are twenty-two. Financial independence from parents, likewise, is elusive.[4]

In younger adults, Barna Group's senior vice president Brooke Hempell sees a connection between loneliness and the expectations they feel. "Now," Hempell says, "you're supposed to go and be Someone, go off to college, go get your advanced degree, go be a leader, go start up a company at age twenty-five—all the things. That's just about attaining success."[5] And it isn't about belonging. It's understood you'll be alone as you pursue these things, even if your funding comes from loved ones.

What's not on the list of things that young people think qualify them for adulthood? Most strikingly, marriage and children. A majority (55%) of young people consider these incidental to adulthood rather than rites of passage into it. Only a quarter (26%) of young adults think moving out of one's parents' household is an essential mark of adulthood.[6]

Transitions that used to be predictable and fairly short—a few years at most—have been extended. In 1975, 45 percent of young adults had lived away from their parents, married, lived with a child, and joined the labor force by age thirty-four. In 2016, only a quarter (24%) had. These life events still generally happen for people today, but much later.[7]

Rather than get married in their twenties as previous generations did, young people today are more likely to stay with their parents. In 2015, about 15 percent of people ages twenty-five to thirty-four were living with a partner, while 40 percent were living with a spouse. This is a big change from 1968, when less than 1 percent of people in that age group were living with a partner and 82 percent were living with a spouse.[8]

Now, however, young adults' expectations are different. Hempell says this represents a completely different life pattern from the oldest generations—even taking into account the upheavals of Boomers' and Elders' youth. Elders, who came of age right after World War II, would graduate from high school and then plan to get a job to support their family of origin or—shortly after that—their own family. Hempell adds that they had a clear focus on work "or getting called into military service of some sort—which they really did view as a service."

Boomers came of age in the 1960s, "experiencing either the Vietnam War or civil rights movement," Hempell notes. There was a lot of unrest in their youth, "but there was still that duty of provision for your family."

Hempell goes on to say, "I recall the mental health crisis of Gen X being a really big deal, because we'd never noticed it before." She believes that a lot of Gen X's emotional crisis had to do with the transition into adulthood. "It was kids who had more and more opportunity than they had seen in previous generations, and there was a sense of lack of purpose." They were asking themselves, "'What am I supposed to do?'" Hempell says, and each generation has felt that crisis of direction more strongly.

Hempell relates that Barna data about Millennials reveals that they're overwhelmed with the sense that "'I'm supposed to be living my best life. I'm supposed to be having all this purpose, and I just don't know what it is.' It's this incredible opportunity before them, and yet it's overwhelming." They simultaneously feel a sense of responsibility to a family they intend to form in the future, Hempell says. "In data we have from a Thrivent study,[9] you had this sense of concern amongst college students about providing for their family. Well, they don't even have a family yet. But they were really worried about it."

Gen Z, the youngest generation of adults, has had some reversals of opportunity and wealth. But the push for college and completing one's education before marriage is still very much a factor.

College freshmen often feel lonely, just one demonstration of how quality and not quantity of relationships matters most.[10]

During transitions, we often feel at loose ends, like those dangling blades of red algae. But what if you had intended to go to college to fulfill your destiny and your destiny suddenly gets yanked away?

The COVID-19 pandemic led to the closure of many college campuses and to many people delaying the next step in their education. Will it also delay adulthood for them? What would it be like for so many people in their twenties to consider themselves not-quite-adults because of delayed education?

A quarter of young people (ages eighteen to thirty-four) lived with their parents in 2016. The COVID-19 pandemic pushed that proportion way up—all the way to a majority (52%) of eighteen- to twenty-nine-year-olds. This isn't unprecedented. It probably also happened during the Great Depression.[11]

Of the many adults now living with their parents, most work or attend school. A quarter do neither, and a quarter have a disability. Many of these adults living with parents are also bringing along their own children, forming multigenerational households.[12]

This could be a nurturing situation for young adults. In Barna's *Households of Faith* report, a study with Lutheran Hour Ministries, mothers came out as a household's "providers of support and drivers of faith formation."[13] Mothers are commonly teenagers' and young adults' confidantes.

However, moving back in with one's parents during the pandemic seems not to have helped with young people's loneliness. In the spring of 2020, 29 percent of those who changed households during the pandemic (because of living in a different household, someone else moving in, or someone moving out) said they always felt lonely, at about three times the rate (9%) of those who had not changed households. Only 28 percent of those in changed households had not felt lonely in the past week, compared to 51 percent of those living in the same household.

Long-term, living with parents doesn't seem to help with wealth either.[14] And while a college education is still a reliably worthwhile financial investment,[15] it comes with debt. What are we to make of this?

My hypothesis is that even when it's absolutely the best practical choice, living with one's parents as a single adult causes a gap in hoped-for bonds. Some cultural groups in the United States are more used to multigenerational families, but you're still more likely to hear jokes about the boomerang generation than to hear respect for them. Young adults, in theory, would rather be financially stable in their early twenties and forming new households in their midtwenties. Do they feel lonely until they leave the in-between status of adult dependents? Is the loneliness of this group explained by their lack of spouses? Is it because of their slipping socioeconomic status? Or is it that they lose some social momentum, stop meeting new people, and stop investing in friendships when they are with their parents?

Most likely the truth is a complicated mess of all these factors under the headings of unmet expectations and uncertain belonging.

Less Time with Friends

I was pretty responsible in high school, but I also remember spending a lot of time driving around in my friend Lily's purple BMW Z3 with the top down. If you didn't have a friend whose parents were quite so generous with cars, you still might remember first dates and parties. But don't be too sure your children have those memories.

Any criticism today of young people with their uncontrolled, hormone-driven socializing at all hours may well fall flat. Young adults have been spending less time with their peers, and they have been doing different things when they do socialize.

Since the 1970s, young people have been spending less and less time together. In 1970, half (52%) of twelfth graders got together with their friends every day, but that had dropped by almost half again, to 28 percent, by 2010.[16] Party-going was drastically down, as was driving in cars for fun, dating, going to the mall, and going to movies. Those people who were teens in the 2010 data on socializing are now adults—adults already past the age when they were hoping to be independent and forming new households.

A winter 2020 survey by Barna showed 33 percent of Millennials saying they spent time with friends before 6:00 p.m. every day, and a smaller proportion saying they spent time with friends when the workday was over, after 6:00 p.m. It may seem a stretch to see a friend every day, but don't expect young adults to make up for all of that on the weekends—51 percent of Millennials spent time during the day with friends less than once a week, and 44 percent of Millennials said they spent an evening with friends less than once a week. For younger adults, in Gen Z, the proportions were similar.

They still spend more time with friends, both during and after work hours, than older adults, according to the winter 2020 Barna survey. Each subsequent generation is less likely to spend time with friends every day and more likely to spend time with friends less than every week—with the exception of the oldest generation, who socialize somewhat more than Boomers.

Still, the change in the way young people socialize will likely have lifelong repercussions. Sharon Hargrave says those high school years are "a developmental stage when you're determining who you are," but now "it's more typical for a young high school kid to go home after school and spend time in their bedroom on a device instead of actually interacting with people." It's a shift away from the sorts of interactions that give you real-life feedback (rather than social media feedback, which is a different sort). People's social skills, and their ability to process and understand interactions, can atrophy. So can the ability to have intimacy in relationships. Young people in their bedrooms on their devices are "not experiencing shared experiences with other young people. They're not experiencing learning together and growing together. They're not forming identity. And so, when we have a lack of a formation of our identity, we don't know who we are, and we're going to be very lonely," Hargrave reports.[17]

Time spent with friends seems to help strengthen young people against the pain of rejection. This combination of factors might mean that young people are in a vicious cycle of lack of company, loneliness, vulnerability to rejection, and low-quality friendships.

The Truth in the Myth: Disability and Bereavement

While there are some individual cases of devastating loneliness among senior citizens, they don't represent the overall pattern. Still, certain experiences that predictably lead to loneliness, such as physical disability and widowhood, are more common in old age. There is an uptick in loneliness among Americans closer to the end of life than to retirement.

Another study found that in both puberty and old age loneliness peaks as "changes in the social environment are also accompanied by major physical and psychological developmental shifts."[18] Our bodies and their capabilities affect how we conduct relationships. Frailty can be as hard to manage as new maturity.

Almost two in five US adults over sixty-five have some sort of disability, according to the US Census Bureau. Most of these have to do with getting around and independent living, things like walking and climbing stairs. Those disabilities are disproportionately among those with a high school education or less, who are poor, and who live alone. They also have a geographical concentration in the Bible Belt.[19]

Many people who have lost mobility find it difficult or impossible to socialize like they used to when they were healthier. They may need help to get out of the house. They may find that it's so time-consuming to go out and come back that they're left with little time to enjoy company. They may feel bad about the help they need and decide not to ask for more than is absolutely necessary.

The man I mentioned at the beginning of the chapter who was wandering around DC trying to assuage the loneliness of little old ladies whom he perceives as in need of companionship isn't likely to encounter this group. He's likely to encounter independent and mobile older women, who tend not to feel lonely very often.

Another shove toward loneliness that many older adults experience is the loss of a spouse. Fewer than one in a hundred Americans is widowed before the age of forty-five. After that, the proportion slowly climbs, hitting 12 percent at age sixty-five and 58 percent by age eighty-five. One in five seniors has been widowed.[20]

This trend hits women much harder, as women generally live longer than men. Thirty percent of women over sixty-five have been widowed, and so have almost three-quarters (72%) of women eighty-five and older.

It's not just spouses who die; friends and siblings die too. But a spouse's death affects daily life and interactions more than others. Spouses are often links to other relationships and initiators of socializing outside the marriage. Spouses come to share memories, and this becomes increasingly valuable when words and memories get harder to access quickly.

Focus on Transitions and Bereavement

Loneliness can strike at any life stage, but it tends to get us during transitions. In the United States right now, the biggest transition is entering adulthood. It's long and difficult and has an end point that is moving out of many young people's reach.

Some but not all of us experience a second big transition of losing physical independence and lifelong partners. We live in a wonderful time, when retirement isn't closely linked to the end of life or to an inability to work. While loneliness seems to be something that fades across generations—and in general it does—that second transition is enough to produce a little burst of loneliness among the very old demographic group. But it's not age that's the issue.

We need to refocus our efforts to combat loneliness on the groups that are actually suffering most. Leaders protect against loneliness by targeting phases of transition and bereavement.

If we focused on people in transitions—whether into or out of independence and marriage—we would make much more headway against loneliness. We might find loneliness reduced across ages.

I'll talk more about marriage in the next chapter, but bereavement belongs here.

People who have lost a spouse will almost always pass through a time of loneliness. Grief just can't be avoided. To keep it from persisting for years and years, a bereaved person has to lean into other intimate friendships and long-term relationships. If one spouse helped the other get out of the house and socialize, then something or someone else must be a motivation to go be with other people. No one can become an old, intimate friend in a matter of days. But we can all make sure that we're paying attention to old friends, staying in contact as they grieve, and both inviting them and saying yes to their invitations for in-person time.

Even something that seems as nonrelational as accessible architecture might be worth a place in a campaign against loneliness. Andy Crouch and Ryan Frederick both mention having accessible public spaces and ease of getting out of the house.

Ryan Frederick is the founder and CEO of SmartLiving 360, which helps prepare for real estate development that takes aging into account, allowing people to thrive where they are, even when, for example, they can't safely step into a bathtub. Frederick says, "There are tangible ways that we can improve physical isolation. Loneliness is just more complicated," but architecture that addresses disability and isolation indirectly addresses loneliness.[21] Leaving the house might lead to talking to the neighbors, buddy time, and the sense of relational security many of us lack (or will lack) because of diabetes, lost vision, or a driver's license we can't renew.

The ways that we can come alongside someone who is grieving are the same ways that we form and deepen friendship otherwise. There are many programs that people, especially seniors, can join. If your bereaved friend doesn't want to join a program, what about walking together, coming over to play cards, or just reading and drinking tea side by side?

Consider the good that you can do all around by helping others. It can mean delivering Meals on Wheels or, like Jimmy Carter, helping build Habitat for Humanity houses. It can also mean babysitting grandkids together or meeting up to help a third friend organize her closets.

MYTH: Older adults are the loneliest.

CORRECTION: Young adults are the loneliest.

THE TRUTH IN THE MYTH: Some things that go with older age (disability and bereavement) do make people lonelier.

CONCLUSION: Generational differences in life structure and life events make young people vulnerable to chronic loneliness. Spending our efforts on transitions and disability will help far more lonely people than a focus on older adults.

4

ROMANCE

MYTH: People who have found true love aren't lonely.

Caelene Peake is the sort of woman who will be on the dance floor at a Bollywood-themed party. She grew up on the coast of South Africa, where the clouds pour over the mountains like liquid nitrogen. When she was a child, her father would take her and her brother out on a boat. They would spend the day swimming, running around on the beaches, and living a Santa Barbara-meets-Boulder lifestyle.

And then she met Jesus. "God gave me an incredible group of sixteen to twenty people who were walking the walk, discipling me, loving me. I was rough around the edges," Peake says, but those friends showed her grace.[1] She was exhilarated by the racially mixed group of Christians so soon after the end of apartheid, by her newfound love of Jesus, and by the urgency of the gospel. "In South Africa, I had deep satisfaction in relationships, all relationships," she says, even though some were significant and some were shallow—and none were perfect.

Within a few years, Peake had married a Texan and moved to Dallas. Not too long afterward, she had a baby and a dream job. It might have looked like she was living an ideal existence, with life stages all on schedule: a nuclear family by her midtwenties.

But she was very, very lonely.

"I gave up everything, all those relationships, as well as those geographical relationships," she says. She and her husband lived near a big intersection full of fast-food joints; instead of waking up to fresh ocean breezes, she smelled the foreign, oily smell of fries. "Loneliness is also compacted by special places—nature, nostalgia, smells—that can be very comforting," she says.

She tried to tough it out. "I was definitely lonely, but I was in total denial about it."

Peake just couldn't find a way to fit in. She tried to joke about buffalo wings and ended up offending buffalo wing aficionados. She sought help for a failing marriage and a colicky newborn and was told, "Now, honey, we don't say things like that around here. We don't say things like that about our husbands." Peake thinks of all those church people she spoke to then and remembers, "I'm basically telling you I'm falling apart, and you're saying what the culture has told you to say. It felt empty."

A nuclear family didn't do the trick, partly because Peake was also in some of the categories that put Americans most at risk for loneliness: young, foreign, and without a confidant. Nuclear family or not, she didn't belong.

It can be easy to blame the loneliness epidemic in the United States on the decline in marriage and dating. It's tempting to believe that if only people could find someone special they would stop being lonely. For better or worse, no family structure will eliminate loneliness. That's because loneliness has to do with the quality of relationships, not just having a person in the role of spouse or being with "the one."

Low-Quality Marriages

Marriage is important for all sorts of things. But even a marriage in which the couple is following Jesus will not necessarily mean the relationship is going to quench either spouse's loneliness. Without love, trust, and communication, marriage doesn't do much for loneliness.

There are many lonely married people. A quarter of married people (26%) in Barna's winter 2020 survey felt lonely every day. According to studies of couples, loneliness tends to hit both spouses rather than leaving one lonely.[2] (Consider that: if you're lonely in your marriage, your spouse is likely to be too.) Unhappy marriages can be more detrimental to happiness and health than no marriage.[3] The quality of a marriage matters more to loneliness than whether a person is married.[4]

Loneliness in marriage goes along with high rates of saying your spouse gets on your nerves, criticizes you, lets you down, and makes too many demands on you. Loneliness in marriage goes along with low rates of saying your spouse understands you and that you can talk about worries and rely on him or her. Sharing a perspective on sex matters too, but not all by itself.[5] Loneliness in marriage also happens when spouses aren't each other's confidants.[6]

Biola University theology professor Matt Jenson says he remembers talking about loneliness with a friend who had married shortly after finishing his education, while Jenson remained single. He says, "I was going through a crushing breakup" and was feeling deeply lonely. His friend, though, sobered him up. "He said you have never known loneliness like the loneliness of lying in bed next to someone and feeling unloved."[7]

There's no effortless transition into a high-quality marriage. You may wear a tux or a white dress and say words of commitment in front of friends and family, but you still find you have to build a good marriage.

And yet the evidence is clear: married people are less lonely than single people. The average marriage protects against loneliness, apparently because the usual marriage is good enough. Marriage is usually a profound experience of belonging and friendship.

Singleness and Loneliness

Single Americans are more likely to be lonely than married Americans. When singles are lonely, they tend to find it more painful than their married counterparts.

In the winter of 2020, single people were more likely to say they were lonely all the time and much less likely—a difference of 18 percentage points—to say they are not lonely than married people (see fig. 4.1). Seventeen percent of single people said they were lonely all the time. That's a higher rate than among married people.

Twenty percent of single people and 17 percent of married people said they were lonely for at least some of each day, but not all the time. Together this means that 38 percent of singles were lonely every day, while among married people the rate was 11 percentage points lower, at 27 percent.[8] A quarter (24%)

Figure 4.1

Frequency of US Adults' Loneliness in Winter 2020 by Marital Status

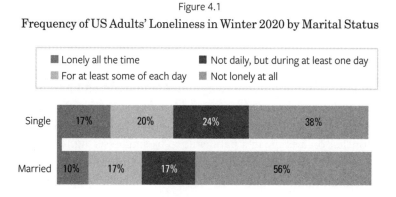

Figure 4.2

Pain of US Adults' Loneliness in Winter 2020 by Marital Status

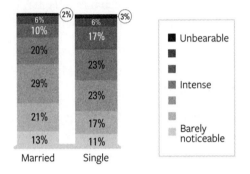

of singles and 17 percent of married people said they had felt lonely during the past week, but not every day.

The biggest gap between married people and single people was in not being lonely. Thirty-eight percent of single people and 56 percent of married people didn't feel lonely at all during the past week.

Of those who are lonely—close to two-thirds of single people, but less than half of married people—the average pain of loneliness is close (see fig. 4.2). Statistically, there's a clear difference, with lonely single people experiencing more pain than lonely married people, but it's only by the difference between a degree easier than "intense" and half a degree easier than "intense."

Singleness in the Pandemic

Social and traditional media are full of reasons why it's difficult in a pandemic to be married with children or to be single without—and everything in between. But the data clearly shows that it's lonelier on average in a pandemic to be single (see fig. 4.3).

In the winter, 56 percent of married US adults and 38 percent of single US adults said they had not felt lonely in the past week.

Figure 4.3

Changes in the Frequency of US Adults' Loneliness between Winter and Spring 2020 by Marital Status

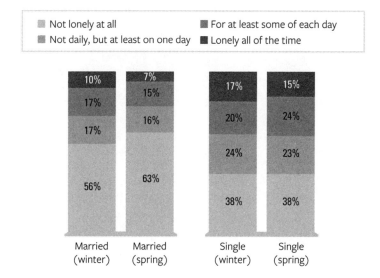

By the spring, that gap had widened; 63 percent of married and 38 percent of single people had not felt lonely. Married people experienced something of a boost.

In the winter, the average (mean) pain of loneliness was significantly higher among single rather than married Americans (see fig. 4.4). In the spring, the average pain of loneliness was not significantly higher among single rather than married Americans. So while both lonely married and lonely single people experienced an increase in their pain, the increase caused lonely married people to "catch up."

Between winter and spring, lonely married people experienced a significant rise in the pain of loneliness, from almost a full step easier than "intense" to somewhat more painful than "intense." Between winter and spring, single people experienced a significant rise in the pain of loneliness, saying

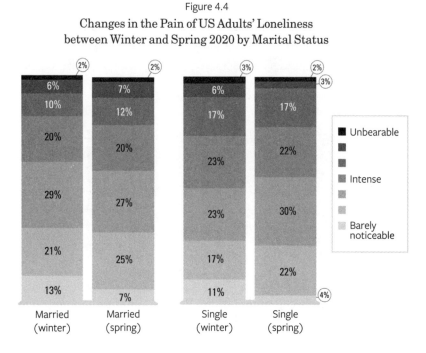

Figure 4.4
Changes in the Pain of US Adults' Loneliness
between Winter and Spring 2020 by Marital Status

on average that their loneliness was a half step worse than "intense."

How are we to understand this? I suspect it has to do with the intensity of what Americans experience in their household. When your household dominates your days, both its benefits and its difficulties are concentrated. So a person in a happy-enough marriage does pretty well with more time at home. But I suspect that married people whose spouses aren't their confidants or buddies find that lack to be more salient when they can't be apart for work and social engagements.

I believe that this data is pointing again to a principle we can see in other dimensions of life: marriage in general, and good marriages in particular, are protective. They help us be resilient, even in something as difficult as a pandemic.

Marriage Delayed or Just Not Happening

If you are married, you are less likely to be lonely. And yet marriage is becoming rarer and is taking place later in life. Younger Americans are less likely to experience its benefits. This is partly because of changing values and lifestyles.

In a US Census report, people ages eighteen to thirty-four in 2012–16 rejected the idea that marriage and children qualify someone for adulthood. Instead, they said accomplishments that are a little more in their control belong before marriage and children in an ideal timeline.[9]

The change in rites of passage has pushed marriage later and later. The average age of those getting married has moved from the early twenties in 1980 to the very late twenties in 2019.[10] Brooke Hempell says, "Normally when you look at national demographics, they change at a snail's pace. So, to have that big of a shift is a huge, huge deal."[11]

It's not that young people are forgoing serious relationships, but the end point of most of them is living together rather than marriage. Now, 9 percent of Americans ages eighteen to twenty-four and 15 percent of Americans ages twenty-five to thirty-four live with a boyfriend or girlfriend.[12] US adults under forty-five are now more likely to have lived with a significant other than to have been married.[13]

Cohabiting might seem pretty similar to marriage. Many cohabiting couples consider themselves to be as committed as married couples, especially if they intend to marry. They might say that marriage is just a piece of paper and that it's love that really binds people. (Though if it's just a piece of paper—why not get it? The answer is most often about wanting financial stability first.)[14]

But cohabitation is different from marriage, and it's not judgmental outsiders who are saying so; people inside cohabiting relationships report different experiences than married people, and their actions also show a difference. Cohabiting couples have less security and satisfaction in their relationships than married couples.[15] Cohabitation doesn't usually lead to marriage. It usually leads to the end of the relationship and to an unstable household for children.[16]

There's some truth to the idea that a piece of paper makes people married, but the piece of paper makes a difference when it comes to a number of things, including loneliness. Cohabiting couples are more like single people than married people when it comes to rates of loneliness.[17]

There's another sad aspect to this: marriage is increasingly something that only well-off couples have, exacerbating inequality—including inequality of loneliness—and perpetuating the difficulties of children born with low socioeconomic status.[18]

In sum, marriage protects against loneliness, but fewer Americans are finding spouses, and when they do, it's later and later. Many wish they were married, but they feel they first must jump a number of unrelated hurdles, most of which are much easier for people when they're already married. On top of this, Americans are dating less and are less able to connect with people they don't already know. It's a recipe for loneliness.

Before rolling our eyes at the careerism or selfishness of single young people, we should stop and ask why these trends are happening. I have personally been accused of selfishness and "delaying marriage" until my midthirties, when in fact I would have dropped just about everything for a good husband. When I met my good husband, I did indeed leave a promising career just when I finally felt I'd gotten some professional traction. And I wasn't alone; only 5 percent of Americans are unmarried and uninterested in marriage.[19] Most adults are either married or hoping to be.

Jenson, who was single until his midforties, once asked his students to think about why the endings of *Romeo and Juliet* and *A Midsummer Night's Dream* are so different when their beginnings are so similar. One student raised a hand and said tentatively, "Fairies?" "Yes!" Jenson said. He compares the serendipity of finding someone to marry to fairy magic. "It was really helpful around my midthirties to realize that people get married for a billion reasons, and it's not much of an achievement to get married. I could have mail-order-bride-ed it." Just as the couples in Shakespeare's comedy find love without any epiphanies or virtues, real couples don't find love or marriage once they are "good enough." Marriage is "irreducibly a gift," Jenson says, "and not a reward."[20]

So, where are those fairies? Why is the consensus that young people should first be finished with their education and financially stable, then married? Why is the consensus that cohabitation before marriage is a good idea? Are these really only the ideas of Millennials, or have Boomers and Gen X peddled them too? Why don't young people feel emotionally or financially prepared for marriage? And then the key question: Why are so many people longing to be married but not finding a match?

Think about the steps it takes to get married. Nearly all of us have to decide we want to marry in general, figure out the sort of person we'd like to marry, meet someone we want to marry, become a person that person wants to marry, commit to an exclusive relationship, reach agreement with that person on the essential parts of life together, commit to an engagement with an end point (a wedding), show up for that wedding, sign those papers, and begin joining our lives.

A failure in any of those steps cuts off the possibility of marriage—for a while at least. Our culture stymies several of those steps and undermines the drive that can get people there. Consider the trend away from face-to-face meeting, the joking-serious messages to men that marriage is the end of all their fun, and pressure on women to look at weddings as their "special day," costing what a four-year degree would.

We've also been sending some counterproductive messages to young people as they transition into adulthood. When we find it embarrassing to talk about marriage with young adults, we undermine the motivation to consider marriage when the considering is good.

When we fail to talk about household economics and the fact that marriage is financially better for each person (particularly for men) than singleness,[21] we encourage the faulty reasoning that financial independence as a single person is a condition of adulthood, whereas it's an unnecessary requirement that often keeps us poor and lonely.

I want to be clear: if anyone starts to push low-quality marriages on young people, thinking it's for their own good, they'll be doing harm instead. Leaders can protect against loneliness by removing the barriers to good marriages, not by facilitating bad marriages. So how can we help people find trustworthy partners? How can we stamp out the lies that people believe about marriage being the same as living together but not as fun? How can we lower the cost of weddings? How can we help young people get financial stability? Answering these questions is one way of helping our lonely culture.

But lowering barriers to good marriage can't stand alone as our only strategy to help reduce loneliness. We must also make singleness better. Some people—many in the next generations— will never marry. The church has always held marriage up, as well it should. But the church has only intermittently honored and supported singleness, although it should have always taken its goodness seriously. Whether churches consider singleness a calling or a circumstance, they can't help singles with loneliness by trying to marry them off their whole lives.

A lack of confidants is one difficulty that often accompanies singleness. Stephanie Holmer is an InterVarsity campus minister at Duke University. She says of singles, "You can come home from work and have no one to debrief with. No one to share the ups and downs and process with. It can be a huge loss."[22] But a bigger loss is often the lack of someone to make big decisions with. This goes beyond the role of confidant and into the role of teammate and adviser.

It shouldn't be necessary to be married to have confidants who are also teammates, advisers, and people to debrief with. Closing the loneliness gap between singleness and marriage means improving the sense of belonging that's available to singles. The single people who show up in churches have the right to expect the same hospitality and warmth that nuclear families receive, even if—especially if—they remain unmarried.

In my research about loneliness, I've often come across a response I think deserves further reflection. The response is along these lines: *It's offensive to say that loneliness and singleness are closely related.*

First of all, this information about loneliness relies on what people say about themselves; it is not a link other researchers or I wanted to exist. One reason we need data is to help us tell the story of a group using their own responses, even when—especially when—it contradicts the story we expect to hear.

Second, I think some people hurt over the link between singleness and loneliness because statistics can seem like fate. But there's no need to fear this. No individual is doomed to loneliness by opinion polling. There will be millions of individual cases of single people who are not lonely, and that may very well include you and the single people you care about.

But most importantly, I want to address hurt feelings by emphasizing that neither loneliness nor singleness is a vice. Neither loneliness nor singleness is a punishment. Loneliness may be a generally negative experience. On a large scale or as a chronic state, it is concerning. But that's very different from saying it's wrong. Similarly, singleness may be disappointing to a lot of people, but that doesn't make it shameful. If someone does find themselves upset by the connection between singleness and loneliness, might it be that they perceive one or both to be shameful? Or if someone feels smug about the connection between loneliness and singleness, might it be that they mistakenly think marriage is a reward for being good? We need to help each other see otherwise.

A Note on Gender and Sexuality

Some anti-loneliness initiatives focus on people who feel rejected or displaced because they are LGBT. The suicide rate in this group is staggering,[23] and people who aren't sexually straight suffer a lot from a lack of belongingness. Most people who identify this way are young, adding to the other sources of loneliness in youth.

People who identified as gay, lesbian, trans, or any other "other" category used to make up a much smaller percentage of young people. But that proportion has risen by a couple percentage points among Millennials in just a few years, from 5.8 percent of Millennials in 2012 to 8.1 in 2016. Young women and people with low incomes are especially likely to identify as something other.[24]

As much as this is a growing group, it is still small, and I do not have enough data to analyze how people in it experience loneliness differently from other groups. What I see from primary and secondary research is that the general principles for leaders in this book also apply to people worried their sexuality or gender will get them rejected.

Jesus makes it clear—as should all Christians—that a relationship with him means belonging in the church and that his forgiveness isn't contingent on being straight. Churches simply must help people following Jesus find a welcome and belonging.

The End of Caelene's Story

Caelene Peake says, "God took me on this long, ten-year journey of loneliness." And then her time in Texas came to an end, as did the biggest of her relationship disappointments.

There was some relief along the way. An older woman had taken a couple effective steps to help. "She said, 'I know you like walking and out-of-doors, and I'm overweight. Let's just walk together,'" Peake says. They started going on walks. When the baby came, her older friend started to sneak into the Peakes' house while Peake and the baby napped. She did laundry, brought vegetables, and then disappeared. Peake felt loved. "This woman is still in my life to this day," she says many years later. "She has always taken the role of encourager."

The biggest difference came when her husband became a Christian. Together, they left their health-and-wealth church for one that didn't blame all problems on someone's lack of faith. They began to repair some of the damage from the first years of their marriage.

Peake is now cofounder of Amazi Water, a charity that brings water wells and safe water to Burundi. She and her husband left the United States for Burundi as a couple who were each other's friends and confidants, and parents who worked together as a team. She would again find herself an outsider and need to form friendships in yet another cultural context. But Peake's crises of loneliness had resolved in many ways.

MYTH: People who have found true love aren't lonely.

CORRECTION: Quality, not type, of relationships keeps people from loneliness.

THE TRUTH IN THE MYTH: Generally, married people are less lonely because marriage often brings real belonging.

CONCLUSION: The average person is less lonely married, and most American adults want to be married. To fight loneliness, we can get to work on removing barriers to marriage. Meanwhile, we—single and married—have to accept prolonged and lifelong singleness in an increased number of adults and start to cultivate belonging in community together.

INSECURITY

MYTH: Poor social skills are the root of loneliness.

In the myth of Pygmalion, a sculptor makes a statue of ideal womanhood, then falls in love with it. Venus brings her to life, and Pygmalion gets to enjoy life with his former statue, Galatea.

Dozens of Pygmalion stories have come out of Hollywood, with one difference: Hollywood Pygmalions fall in love with girls who are dorky, not ivory. Once Hollywood Galateas have contacts and either perms or straightened hair, Pygmalions are ready to officially date them and Pygmalions' friends to accept them. Galateas' lonely days are over. Good thing they are no longer dweebs! Just think of them having to end high school without becoming hot girls.

Pop culture pitches us the idea that belonging is for people who meet certain social requirements, the same set that gets you invited to keggers in college and Sunday brunches afterward. But that's as much a myth as Pygmalion and Galatea. Take it from a mousey, glasses-wearing poetry major whose job involves a lot of statistics: anyone can have the kind of relationships that fend off loneliness most of the time.

(Also: makeovers do not solve loneliness.)

Insecurity and Loneliness

Nevertheless, lonely people often do give off signals of wanting to keep their distance from others. On average, they seem less confident than other people, and they may even be hostile.[1] It's not dorkiness they are suffering from, though. It's insecurity.

Insecurity will keep you from a full life. Those same Pygmalion-themed movies that show makeovers opening the door to a complete life often also portray nerds as a group of outcasts, loosely united by jealousy of popular kids. If they existed, those kids *would* be lonely. They'd be insecure. Their minds would be so attuned to the differences between who they are and who they wish they were that they would actually reject belonging when they could have it.

In real life, such insecurity isn't just at the dorks' cafeteria table. It's everywhere people are preoccupied with rejection. Insecurity follows us from school into adulthood and moves the goal post farther and farther away, keeping us from ever feeling we're valued and safe as we are.

In the second Barna survey on loneliness in the spring of 2020, people answered the question "Think back on the past seven days. How often would you say you felt insecure?" As with the question about loneliness, they indicated whether they felt insecure all the time, for at least some of each day, not daily but during at least one day, or not at all. About half (53%) had not felt insecure at all during the past week.

Similar proportions had felt insecure daily or weekly (19 and 21%). Seven percent had felt insecure all the time. Note that not everyone who is insecure can—or is willing to—name it; I would expect real rates of insecurity to be much higher.

Figure 5.1
Insecurity and Loneliness: Spring 2020

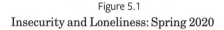

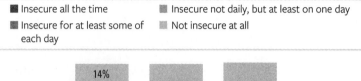

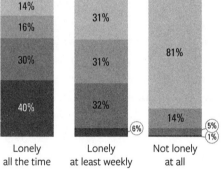

There was a strong link between insecurity and loneliness (see fig. 5.1). Of those who hadn't felt lonely, four in five (81%) hadn't felt insecure either. The pattern holds as the frequency of loneliness goes up. Of those who constantly felt lonely, about two in five constantly felt insecure—almost six times the rate of the general population.

The question about insecurity also revealed other connections to loneliness. Younger Americans were more likely to be insecure, as were unmarried Americans. White Americans were less likely to feel insecure than ethnic minorities.

Injustice, Insecurity, and Loneliness

But it's a myth that social skills are always at the root of loneliness. Many of us have experienced bullying and meanness in our school years. It may have been about our accents or our hair or the age of our parents' car. Some of us have to endure injustice and cruelty in multiple dimensions of our lives—in our families, workplaces, neighborhoods, and more.

Those incidents may feel so bad that even several good things can't make up for them. People tend to feel negative experiences much more deeply than positive experiences. That's why it takes five good interactions for every tough interaction in a marriage to keep a couple happy together.[2] It may well be that most relationships work like that—certainly, the good needs to be far more frequent to outweigh the bad.

But not all relationships are ones in which both sides are trying to get along. Social undermining (the opposite of support) does us a lot of harm, whether it's contempt, discrimination, or some other behavior that shows someone rejects our worth.[3] Whether intentional or not, social undermining quickly leads to loneliness. So often this sort of rejection intersects with injustice.

It might not seem like a straight path from injustice to insecurity to loneliness. But imagine what it might mean to your Black friend when you, a White person, can't bear to say "Black lives matter" for fear of aligning with an organization you dislike. Not saying his life matters is very much like saying he could be murdered for all you care. Wouldn't that make you feel out in the cold?

For Black Americans, who make up about one-seventh of the population, life is generally harder. In 2020, relatively stable levels of crime in White neighborhoods contrasted with spikes in both crime and COVID-19 in Black neighborhoods.[4] These fears, as well as the usual expectation about having résumés tossed because their names sound Black and fears about joining the ranks of Black people killed because others see them as inherently criminal, quite predictably lead to loneliness. And, indeed, Black people in America were lonelier in the winter of 2020.

Some US minorities experience loneliness differently from each other or from the White majority. It is interesting to look at these trends in light of the much greater mortality among Black and Hispanic Americans to COVID-19.

In the winter of 2020, Black Americans (but not multiethnic Americans who were Black and another ethnicity) said they felt lonely all the time at more than twice the rate of White respondents (see fig. 5.2). While the proportions of the three biggest ethnic groups in the United States were similar for daily and weekly loneliness, there were significant differences again for those who had not felt lonely at all. Half (49%) of White and Hispanic respondents had not felt lonely in the past week, but only 37 percent of Black respondents hadn't felt lonely.

Figure 5.2
Changes in the Frequency of US Adults' Loneliness between Winter and Spring 2020 by Ethnicity

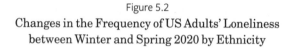

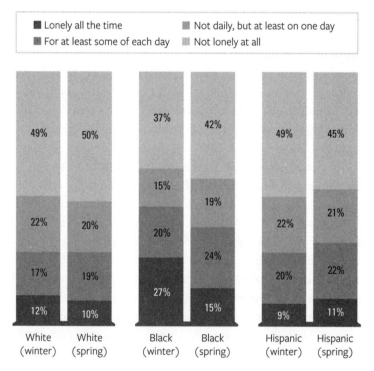

Among those who were lonely, there weren't differences in the average degree of pain White and Black respondents experienced. Loneliness was more painful for Hispanic Americans, however.

Between the winter and the spring of 2020, the pain of loneliness in all ethnic groups rose significantly. The biggest increase was in the biggest group, non-Hispanic White Americans.

Race and ethnicity are entangled with other characteristics. For example, Black Americans tend to experience lower socioeconomic status—something that never really got solved in the post–Emancipation Proclamation years.

Keep in mind that socioeconomic status is often a good substitute for the concept of opportunity. High socioeconomic status means you have some momentum behind your aspirations. Low socioeconomic status means you have friction, making it harder to achieve aspirations and making each failure bring you closer to a real emergency. People are less likely to be lonely when well-educated and wealthy,[5] two factors that usually have to do with socioeconomic status.

Foreigners, like ethnic minorities, also tend to feel lonelier. One study found that the loneliness comes from separation from friends and family, discrimination, language barriers, and more.[6] Both Caelene Peake and Sanyin Siang attest to this. Siang is executive director of Duke University's Coach K Center on Leadership and Ethics. She says, "As an immigrant, I learned very quickly you never feel you're fully a member of the community you've joined. And you never feel you're fully a member of the community you've left."[7]

Sandra Van Opstal is executive director and cofounder of Chasing Justice and author of several books, including *The Next Worship*. Van Opstal says she sees loneliness "being strongly affiliated with being young, single, Black, low income. That's absolutely true for what I'm seeing in my own community, as a neighbor and as a community leader and as a pastor."[8]

Insecurity and Its Distortions

Sometimes insecurity comes from having been discriminated against, having been treated unjustly or unmercifully. But there's another side to it as well.

Insecurity often comes out of a negative way of processing our interactions. We all spend more time than we realize guessing the subtext of what someone else said or did. As a group, humans are pretty self-centered and prone to forget that others are more likely to be thinking about themselves than about us.[9] This is called the Spotlight Effect, ironically; we often mistakenly think others will notice us, as if we were standing in the spotlight.

Sharon Hargrave says, "That feeling of loneliness comes upon us, and we start giving ourselves negative messages on top of that. These messages start piling on."[10] So when we have an interaction that isn't overwhelmingly positive, we tell ourselves stories. Confabulatory stories. Stories about how they are rejecting us in subtle ways.

Those friends who moved a coffee date to the next weekend? Probably can't stand us. Want to hang out with just about anyone else. Wish they had never said yes in the first place. The siblings who haven't responded to our text messages? Probably rolling their eyes right now. They're rejecting our love. The children who told us they won't be coming for Thanksgiving or Christmas this year? They are taking our grandchildren away. Or it's their nasty spouses who have always hated us.

Those of us who know deeply insecure people may be taken aback by the range of things they can take as rejection, from pauses to compliments. They may tell you they've "been burned before," only for you to realize later that the burn-er is a kind and baffled ex-friend.

One study on loneliness throughout life found that lonely people mistrust others in general, and they tend to explain relationships in a way that makes them victims of fate.[11] A lonely person is likelier to seem shy, anxious, awkward, or lower in self-esteem.[12] They may act "innocuously sociable,"[13] smiling and nodding and giving no reason for anyone to reject them. It can be hard to get to know their real thoughts or opinions; that's the point.

On the other hand, lonely people may take a preemptive approach. They want to avoid rejection or exclusion by reject-ing first. Lonely people more often than others project hostil-ity and lack of trust, leading others to enjoy the relationship less.[14] Their expectation of rejection becomes a self-fulfilling prophecy.[15]

So insecurity lives in our imaginations. When our imagina-tions seek out signs of rejection everywhere, they find those signs. They just may not be true at first. Then, as we respond to perceived slights, we may become more difficult for people to be close to.

Compounding the problem, people who are vigilant for signs of rejection find they're depleting their resources for other forms of self-regulation.[16] With low self-regulation, we have difficulty, for example, avoiding a fight, adjusting how long we look at social media, or going to bed on time.

The thirst of loneliness is for relationships in which we feel secure. But insecurity makes our thirst insatiable. We cannot appreciate the good things we have.

One way for lonely people to work against loneliness is to think differently. How might they do so when they have already developed a particular way of viewing the world? It turns out that thinking can be taught—and fairly effectively. The most effective programs for fighting loneliness did so by addressing "maladaptive social cognition"—that is, counterproductive thinking about relationships.[17]

One successful program taught lonely people to "identify automatic negative thoughts and regard them as hypotheses to be tested rather than facts."[18] So when someone in this program found himself thinking, "Those guys will never invite me camping. They only hang out with other athletes," he could then say, "My hypothesis is that those guys only hang out with other athletes. I wonder if that's true." Now he needs to look for disconfirming evidence—that is, for a real-life example of a way that hypothesis isn't true. He could ask, "Is there a case where they've hung out with someone like me?" Or he could ask, "Would they come over if I invited them to a backyard cookout?" To test the hypothesis, he would have to observe or ask about their circle of friends and look for exceptions to his assumption. Or he would have to invite them over and see if they came.

Another study on loneliness throughout life suggested training lonely children to pay attention to context, including good things that can come out of their social environment, and to things other than "social threat."[19] These methods and others like them had the biggest effect on loneliness, compared to programs that taught social skills, tried to get people more connected to support, or tried to connect people at all.[20]

Note, though, that your hypothesis that someone is rejecting you might turn out to be true, and your context might be crummy. It's a good idea to prepare for dealing with real rejection—but that is a different problem than the problem of expecting only harm. The point is to stop assuming that everything is bad, rather than proving to ourselves that everything is good; it's not. We need some fortitude to deal with real relationships.

I don't know where the line falls between the spiritual and the cognitive. But I think it seldom matters all that much. Over and over, Christians are told to invest in self-regulation. That is, we are to be conscious of our thoughts and whether they align with Christ's. We are to pay attention to how well we are setting ourselves up for future temptation (and future glory) by, for example, building up self-control. We are to fight distortions.

None of this is primarily about therapy; it's about spiritual growth.

I believe insecurity always has a spiritual aspect to it—and that security has a spiritual source: our security in Christ. As Christians, we can train our thoughts so that our often-false sense of rejection doesn't metastasize and kill our relationships.

There are ways you can help yourself and others at the same time. Parents, especially fathers, have a huge role to play in helping their children have good thought habits. Sometimes our kids will pick up how we respond without any effort on our part.[21] Often all we have to do is say something out loud about how we changed our mind: "I was worried that someone didn't like me, but when I talked with her, I realized that she was probably just busy. I'll try to get together with her again sometime." Or "I was angry at someone because I thought he had been unkind. I found out today that he hadn't been unkind at all. I was wrong to resent him without first trying to find out if I knew the truth." These things can really stick in a child's mind and be helpful throughout life.

To help lonely adults, leaders will primarily practice, then preach. We must demonstrate a willingness to question our expectations of others and to change our minds about them. How can we teach others to conduct good relationships if ours are riddled with resentment and assumptions? Once we're on the path to security, we can help others along.

In the same Barna survey as the one that asked about loneliness and insecurity, people also answered a question about peace. Peace is, in many ways, the opposite of insecurity. Respondents were able to indicate on a scale from zero to ten how much they agreed that "I have an inner sense of peace, even in difficult circumstances." That sense of peace is strongest in the groups that are least lonely, particularly among older generations and practicing Christians.

Depending on what respondents meant (and here we're guessing), peace can be a synonym for security. When we feel peace, we aren't vigilant. We can broaden our perspective. We can relax and appreciate. We regain perspective. How wonderful that God gives peace as a greeting in a world with so much insecurity.

Peace is one of the marks of someone who is following Jesus. Peace fights loneliness.

We can help create a more trustworthy society by practicing justice and mercy on both an individual level and a much bigger level. While we can't make anyone else feel secure, we can strive to make our communities and our country into a place where people don't have their expectations of racism met with racism, their disadvantage met with further disadvantage, or their assailants met with impunity.

As Van Opstal says, "Biblical justice is lived out in the life of a Christian who's asking the questions, 'How do I bring restoration?' 'How do I bring flourishing?'"[22] That effort brings a Christian deeper into a purposeful pursuit of a less lonely society.

Justice and mercy fight loneliness.

So do welcome, acceptance, and inclusion.[23]

MYTH: Poor social skills are at the root of loneliness.

CORRECTION: People are lonely when they are insecure or have low status, whether from discrimination or for another reason.

THE TRUTH IN THE MYTH: Sometimes people are insecure because they expect and see negative interactions.

CONCLUSION: Fighting loneliness means removing true unfairness, but it also means addressing thought habits.

6

SOCIAL MEDIA

MYTH: People are lonely because they spend too much time on social media.

With the rise of social media, a new creature came into being: influencers. Serious influencers, many with wisdom and good intentions, have amassed social media followers in the tens or hundreds of thousands—or even millions.

But lifestyle influencers are a different breed. They can be found poolside, hiking, or in hotels most of us can't afford. If they're boys, they engage in "antics." If they're girls, they seem to be either doing their hair or traveling. They are invariably good looking and have better legs and bigger hats than the rest of us. Remarkably, they don't seem to need jobs. That's because the biggest influencers receive tens or even hundreds of thousands of dollars per post from advertisers.[1]

Lifestyle influencers are often modeling a life that is almost entirely aspirational. An occasional confessional about suffering or reminder that even influencers can get hurt brings a soupçon of reality to their media accounts.

Of course, all people are real people, influencers or otherwise. But not all the lives people portray are real; many social media accounts are scripted and curated just as surely as a TV show is. Unfortunately, it's hard for many of us to remember those lives are distortions for the sake of advertising or entertainment.

Influencers do it, but so do our friends. Their Instagram photos are of highlights; they're not really letting us in. The less we see them in person, the easier it is to take others' posts as typical. Sandra Van Opstal describes using social media for ministry: "Hey, I'm just trying to make a difference in the world. But it seems like I can't keep up with what everybody else is doing. Probably a lot of people are feeling, 'I'm not doing as well as they are. I'm not as happy as they are. I'm not as successful as they are. I'm not as important or relevant as they are.'"[2]

At least, that's how the story goes. Ask someone what is making people lonely and you're likely to hear "social media." Remarkably, that answer is both true and false.

Loneliness and Social Media

Social media apps and websites are as constant as air for young Americans. More than three-quarters of young adults ages eighteen to twenty-four use Snapchat, Instagram, YouTube, and Facebook daily.[3] Daily users are generally more-than-once-a-day users.[4]

Research looking at how digital communication affects youth supports the idea that it accompanies increased *and* decreased loneliness. Yes, as a group, young people have experienced increased loneliness as their social media use has risen.[5] That's a concern for the generations to come, and possibly for older generations as they begin to use social media more often. But, when looking at individuals, social media use isn't as big a problem as many expect. That's because the young people who use social media also see others in person the most. Seeing others face-to-face protects against loneliness.

Take away the face-to-face time, and young people who use social media at high rates are lonelier.[6] There are, of course, people who socialize little and use social media a lot. They may find that being more deliberate about their social media use can help them feel less anxious.[7]

Still, like any tool, social media can be misused. Sharon Hargrave credits a "large portion of loneliness" to "*unhealthy* use of social media. Social media itself is not the only contributor to loneliness, but it is when used incorrectly [that] it has created problems."[8]

"The difference between using media strictly supplementally versus in a primary way is really central," says Andy Crouch, author of several books, including *The Tech-Wise Family*. Crouch notes that Jesus and the early church seem not to have used the technology available to them.[9] "Jesus himself did not use media—if media is anything that comes in the middle between two persons and substitutes for some aspect of embodied communication. Jesus never wrote anything down that we have a record of." And as for the early church, "we don't have any evidence that any of the canonical letters were put in the postal service; they were sent with a person. So, Phoebe carries Romans to Rome. The mediated component of the communication is accompanied by a personal component—which, incidentally, they also did with money."

Neither money nor correspondence was something they let stand on its own as "a primary vector of relationship," Crouch says. Those were supplemental and accompanied by a person.

This isn't necessarily a question of right and wrong, but it does point to a principle for forming and maintaining relationships; supplement with lower-quality interactions, like video calls or text messages, but the main part of a relationship needs to be high-quality, in-person time.

Fear of Missing Out and Loneliness

Some loneliness is caused by fear of missing out (FOMO). This fear can drive some people to distraction, particularly if they feel they are being pushed out of an inner circle.

People who have a problem with FOMO often agree with statements like "I get anxious when I don't know what my friends are up to" and "I fear others have more rewarding experiences than me." They tend to use social media more frequently than other people do. Fear of missing out might seem laughable, but it's a form of distress.

Because of this, researchers have wondered if there is a link between FOMO, social media use, and loneliness. Experiments are the primary way to clearly show causes and effects. That's because they even out all the other characteristics people have, make sure the order of events (cause, then effect) is clear, and more. Otherwise, we can look at patterns and make educated guesses. But to know whether social media causes loneliness, we need a way of finding out if very similar groups of people get lonelier when they use more social media and if they get less lonely when they use less social media.

One experiment assigned college students either to continue using social media on Facebook, Instagram, and Snapchat as usual or to limit each to ten minutes per day.[10] The intervention was a success. The students who were told to limit their social media use reported lower levels of loneliness and depression after the three-week experiment.

But the other group, who used social media as usual, also experienced an improvement in loneliness and depression. Even though their results were outstripped by the ten-minutes-per-platform group, it seems that just paying attention to how much we use social media can make us healthier. And that may be particularly true for those of us who are worried we'll miss something if we stop looking.

Finding Balance

When I asked Brooke Hempell if people look to social media to feel known, she answered emphatically: "No, they go to create their identity, not to be genuinely known."[11]

She says people might not even be aware of what they're doing, but some are. "People will have multiple identities on social media to represent different areas of their life or different things that they are involved with," and it starts to seem like they're split into different people. "It feels like I know people, but I don't really know them—and in fact that's not what we're here [on social media] for. We're not here to get to know each other and be vulnerable. We're here to show the best of ourselves and to build up an image of ourselves."

I asked Hempell who really knows young people, particularly when they have multiple identities on social media. She responded, "I don't know that they know that they need to have that." She says some people may have friends who really understand them, but "parents are less likely to have that connection."

There is an exception. "When we did the Gen Z research, we saw that a certain group of youth did have that relationship with their parents. They tended to be those youth who were really also connected with the church. They had a strong conversational relationship with their parents; they would talk to them about tough topics, and that was healthy and good," Hempell says. "But then we saw that those that didn't have the church connection also weren't having relational connections with their families in that way."

Many people have called for authenticity online. The argument is that we mislead each other by posting only highlights of our lives, or the parts that make us look good. I disagree. Posting about the raw parts of life doesn't suddenly make everything better—or even more balanced. Turning a camera on our child as he throws a tantrum or alluding to a recent fight in a Facebook post can actually make things worse in person, off social media. We do need to protect our relationships and others' privacy.

So what's to be done about our social media accounts? First of all, by no means be deceptive. Second, pay attention to what you know is wise, not what you hope will be popular. When you find that you've somehow inspired envy, some might say the best course is to hide your light.

Don't hide your light! It's envy-ers, not objects of envy, that cause envy. Of course, if we know others are jealous of us, we should make sure we're not actually being unkind or doing anything wrong.

Beyond that, we can make social media less about our charmed lives and more about appreciation and connection. We often can invite people to enjoy what we're enjoying, whether visually or in person. We can mix up posts about our lives with cute puppy photos or something that inspires awe and wonder.

But don't imagine there's much to be done when someone is jealous of your motorcycle or your husband. Those people will likely see your appreciative posts as smarmy anyway.

The clearest way to protect ourselves from the harm of social media is to balance it with in-person time. A second way is to limit the time we spend on social media. Another way is to track the time we spend on social media.

Each of those is easy to do with a little effort, particularly up front. You can use parental controls on your devices to limit your time on social media. You can book buddy dates and make sure your phone is off. You can monitor your social media use on most devices without even changing your settings.

As always, as leaders we need to set an example. We can recommend spending a greater proportion of time with people and articulate why. And the great thing is that many in our circles will already be balancing social media with buddy time.

MYTH: People are lonely because they spend too much time on social media.

CORRECTION: Many people who use social media a lot also see people in person a lot, protecting them from loneliness.

THE TRUTH IN THE MYTH: In general, social media use and loneliness have grown together. FOMO, social media apart from in-person relationships, and jealousy do make people lonely, and we can use social media in a way that exacerbates these.

CONCLUSION: Social media are tools, and when we use them to supplement healthy in-person relationships, they're fairly safe. When we use them to replace those relationships or allow their distortions to alter how we think of our lives and relationships, we can find ourselves lonelier for using them.

7

FAITH AND CHURCHGOING

MYTH: Going to church makes people less lonely.

What do we expect from churches? Whatever your Christian beliefs, they likely include the idea of community. In fact, churches
look like such a good model of community that non-Christian
groups have deliberately imitated them.

The benefits of church are compelling. Larger and more satisfying social networks must be close to the top of the list of
benefits.[1] But there's also the increase in life expectancy; the
more regularly you go to church, the more likely you are to get
a few more years.[2] If you get breast cancer, you are less likely
to die from it.[3] Middle-aged churchgoers who routinely attend
worship services sleep better.[4] According to one researcher,
church "boosts the immune system."[5]

Longer life, better sleep, improved immunity, lower likelihood of heart trouble,[6] less depression and stress—these sound
like the mirror image of loneliness's symptoms. It seems like
church should make people less lonely and even that it might be
a direct response. However, in the winter of 2020, churchgoers
were lonely about as frequently as Americans in general and
slightly more often than those who didn't go to church.

Churchgoing and Loneliness

Christians who go to church and say their faith is important to them—that is, practicing Christians—are slightly more lonely than the many Christians who aren't practicing.

Barna identified practicing Christians in the winter and spring of 2020 as those who said they were Christians, who attended a religious service at least once in the past six months, and who said their faith was very important. Nonpracticing Christians self-identified as Christians but did not fit the profile for "practicing" because of attending church infrequently and/or not agreeing strongly that their faith was very important in their lives. Non-Christians did not self-identify as Christians.

The difference in the results wasn't in how many people were lonely at all; for all groups, that was just under half—46 percent of practicing Christians and non-Christians, and 47 percent of nonpracticing Christians (see fig. 7.1). However, practicing

Figure 7.1

Frequency of Loneliness in Winter 2020 by Christian Practice

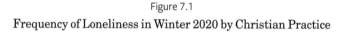

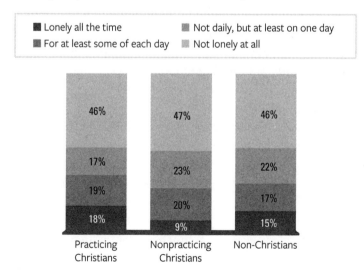

Christians said they were lonely all the time at twice the rate of nonpracticing Christians (18%, compared to 9%).

And then things changed. US adults' faith and practice made a bigger difference in their experience of loneliness as the pandemic altered life.

Before COVID-19, practicing Christians had reported fairly normal frequencies of loneliness. Between the winter and spring of 2020, practicing Christians became far less likely to say they had experienced loneliness. Other religious groups, nonpracticing Christians, and non-Christians had very similar rates of loneliness in the winter and spring.

This is remarkable since, according to other Barna research, about a third of practicing Christians (32%) had already stopped attending church services by early May, when many churches met online.

In the spring of 2020, 60 percent of practicing Christians—a leap of 14 percentage points from the winter of 2020—said they had not been lonely in the past week. This was the biggest change in loneliness according to Christian practice. In the corresponding groups, there was little change: 46 percent of nonpracticing Christians, and 43 percent of non-Christians had not been lonely in the past week in the spring of 2020 (see fig. 7.2). The proportion of practicing Christians who had been lonely not daily but during the week didn't change, at about one in five people. That was very similar to the proportions of non-practicing Christians and non-Christians.

The proportion of practicing Christians who had been lonely daily dropped during the early pandemic, from 19 percent to 11 percent in the spring of 2020, while the rate among nonpracticing Christians stayed the same and the rate among non-Christians increased.

Eighteen percent of practicing Christians said they experienced the most extreme frequency of loneliness—feeling lonely "all the time"—in the winter of 2020. By spring, this

Figure 7.2

Changes in the Frequency of US Adults' Loneliness between Winter and Spring by Christian Practice

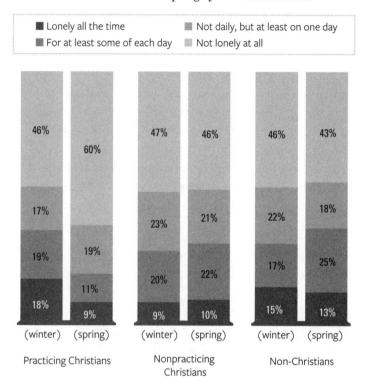

had dropped to half the rate (9%). This, however, was less an advantage for practicing Christians than an equalizing trend, bringing them in line with the proportion of nonpracticing Christians who felt lonely all the time. In the spring of 2020, 10 percent of nonpracticing Christians and 13 percent of non-Christians said they felt lonely all the time—not a significant change for either group. So we see practicing Christians saying as the pandemic set in that they were less lonely, while other religious groups stayed the same.

Loneliness was more painful on average after the pandemic had begun (see fig. 7.3). By May, lonely Americans were reporting an increase in the pain of loneliness. Lonely practicing Christians were no exception, and for them, the rise was steeper than for other religious groups. Lonely practicing Christians said they experienced less than the usual amount of pain from loneliness in the winter of 2020, but by spring of 2020 they had a very similar level of pain to other religious groups.

Practicing Christians may not hold orthodox beliefs, but their faith is important enough to them and they show up at least occasionally.

Barna did ask more specific questions about beliefs as well. These surveys were able to categorize people as "born again" if they answered yes to "Have you ever made a personal commit-

Figure 7.3
Changes in the Pain of US Adults' Loneliness
between Winter and Spring 2020 by Christian Practice

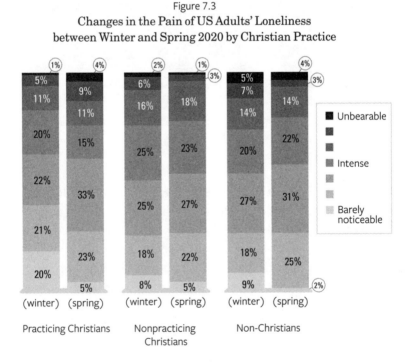

ment to Jesus Christ that is still important in your life today?" and indicated that after dying "I will go to heaven because I have confessed my sins and have accepted Jesus Christ."

During the winter of 2020, there weren't significant differences in the rate of loneliness between the born-again and the not born-again groups (see fig. 7.4). But by the spring, there was a significant difference between the percentage of born-again and not born-again respondents who had not felt lonely in the past week (57% versus 45%). The difference is due to the rising proportion of born-again Christians who had not felt lonely.

In the winter and the spring of 2020, lonely born-again and not born-again respondents had almost the same average pain of loneliness.

Figure 7.4

Changes in the Frequency of US Adults' Loneliness between Winter and Spring 2020 by Born-Again Beliefs

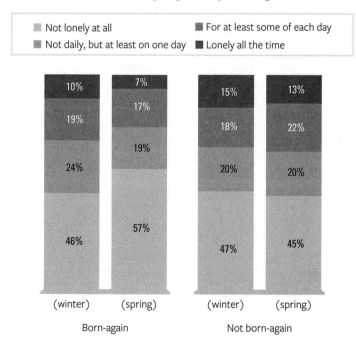

So practicing Christians and born-again Christians had a surprising boost during the pandemic. How can we explain this?

Stigma against Loneliness

What if they underreported their loneliness because they want to be "good"? They may believe that Christians ought not to be lonely, for example. Because of that, they may have put the "right" answer on the survey, indicating that they felt lonely far less than they actually did.

As I mentioned in chapter 1, there are reasons to believe that practicing Christians think it might be bad to feel lonely. And while the evidence isn't conclusive, this seems to be plausible after checking into it.

Fifteen percent of practicing Christians said loneliness is always embarrassing, at three times the rate of non-Christians (5%) and twice the rate of nonpracticing Christians (8%). This embarrassment might have caused some practicing Christians to deny their loneliness. Even on anonymous surveys, many people don't tell the truth. And if something is completely embarrassing, how likely are you to admit to it—even to yourself?

A quarter of practicing Christians (25%) said loneliness is always bad, compared to 18 percent of nonpracticing Christians and 19 percent of non-Christians. If something is always bad, do you enjoy identifying with it?

Does this mean practicing Christians are actually much lonelier than the general population? Or are their responses as accurate as other religious groups'? That we don't know. Unfortunately, in this case, a survey cannot do more than tell us whether people think one answer is a better people pleaser.

There is some truth in the idea that faithful Christians are lonelier. The data we have confirms it—they were more likely than nonpracticing Christians to feel constantly lonely before the pandemic. But still, we should take what people say about themselves seriously. This data shows that even with the world trying to isolate people during a pandemic, practicing Christians experienced a boost, becoming less lonely than both non-Christians and nonpracticing Christians. That indicates a good deal of resilience, and maybe even some anti-fragility. What might be behind this, in addition to spiritual factors?

Advantages of Church Attendance

People practicing other religions get some of the same boost that practicing Christians get. Just like a balanced diet and exercise, these advantages work pretty much the same across religions.

People who attend church are probably at an advantage when it comes to friendship. When you go to church regularly, you generally meet people and make friends. While in some churches there is little turnover, other churches have fresh faces frequently, with new opportunities for friendship. Right off the bat, you know that you have a common interest in God or faith. When the going gets tough, your church will certainly be trying to gather people (even if virtually, as during the pandemic).

Face-to-face time with friends protects against loneliness. Practicing Christians do spend time during the day with friends more often than nonpracticing Christians do. It's the same with church attenders (a group that includes practicing Christians but where members may or may not say their faith is very important to them). They are more likely to spend time with other people during the week, and not just once a week; their rate of seeing friends every day before 6:00 p.m. (30%) is more than twice the rate as among unchurched people (12%), and their rate of seeing friends every evening is similarly about two times as frequent (20%, compared to 9%).

Sandra Van Opstal says that young people who are active in churches stay connected, even if only through video calls because of the pandemic. "If you're connected to a faith community, you have people that are checking in on you. You might make meals for one another. There's a group of people that remember your birthday, not just because Facebook told you so."[7]

Group singing is another big advantage. That's right—group singing is a real force for unity and belonging. When people sing together, they feel included and connected. They release endorphins, stress-reducing hormones.[8] So if a group asks you to join them in singing and chanting, expect to bond a bit in the process.

Practicing Christians are somewhat more likely than other Americans to be older and married, further reducing their likelihood of loneliness.

All of these advantages point in the direction of less loneliness even in non-pandemic times, despite the self-reports that practicing Christians didn't have a big advantage until the pandemic.

Meaning in Life

Meaning in life is another link between churchgoing and loneliness. In the winter of 2020, respondents rated whether they agreed with the statement "I have what I need to live a meaningful life" (see fig. 7.5). The wording is vague so that they could supply their own idea of what it means to have a meaningful life. To some, it may mean leaving a legacy. To others, it may mean getting to do what they love as a career. To others, it may mean raising children or staying positive or following Jesus Christ.

The question prompted them to think. What do they need—and do they already have it? Do they need a certain amount of money? To be married? To understand the Bible?

Most people find that they do have what they need. In other words, they can live with purpose. Nothing is keeping them from what's really important.

People who attend church at least somewhat regularly were more likely to agree with the statement "I have what I need to live a meaningful life." In the winter of 2020, 43 percent agreed strongly, and another 36 percent agreed somewhat, so that 79 percent of churchgoers said they have what they need to live a meaningful life. Fourteen percent were in the middle, and the remaining 6 percent disagreed.

That's a much different profile than that of US adults who do not attend church often, whether or not they identify as Christians. While a majority agreed they have what they need to live a meaningful life, a fifth (22%) were in the middle, and 4 percent said they didn't know. Twelve percent of non-churchgoers disagree that they have what they need to live a meaningful life. That means one in eight unchurched Americans doesn't think a meaningful life is immediately available.

Meaning is not only connected to churchgoing, it is also connected to loneliness. The connection, though, isn't a straight line, where one increases and the other decreases steadily.

Figure 7.5

Agreement with "I Have What I Need to Live a Meaningful Life" in the Winter of 2020 by Church Attendance

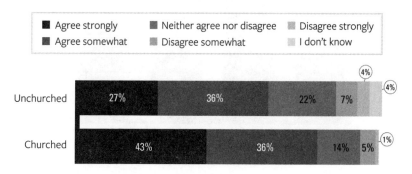

People who were never lonely were very likely to say they agreed they have what they need to live a meaningful life, with 41 percent agreeing strongly and 40 percent agreeing somewhat (see fig. 7.6). Fourteen percent were in the middle, neither disagreeing nor agreeing. About 3 percent disagreed somewhat or strongly, and 2 percent said they didn't know.

People who were lonely weekly or daily didn't reflect the same certainty about meaningful lives. The proportion that agreed strongly dropped to about a quarter, 22 percent for those who were lonely weekly and 24 percent for those who were lonely daily. Those who were lonely weekly agreed somewhat at about the same rate as those who weren't lonely—41 percent. Those who were lonely daily had a lower proportion agreeing somewhat (31%). Both groups were far more likely to put

Figure 7.6

Agreement with "I Have What I Need to Live a Meaningful Life" in the Winter of 2020 by Frequency of Loneliness

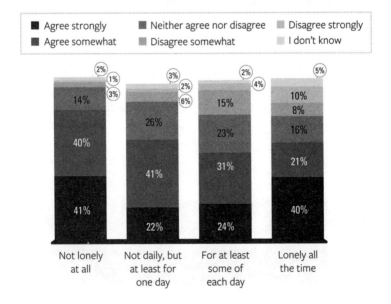

themselves in the middle, with about a quarter in each group neither agreeing nor disagreeing. Eight percent of those lonely at least weekly and 19 percent of those who were lonely every day disagreed strongly or somewhat that they have what they need to live a meaningful life. A low percentage (2 and 3%) said they didn't know.

The surprise is people who said they were always lonely. This group agreed strongly that they have what they need to live a meaningful life at about the same rate as the group that hadn't been lonely in the past week (40%). This group was less likely to say they agreed somewhat (21%) and similarly likely to say they neither agreed nor disagreed (16%). This group was the most likely to disagree strongly that they have what they need to live a meaningful life (10%), but not much more likely to disagree somewhat (8%).

In other words, lonely people are more likely than those who are not lonely to have a hard time seeing how they'll live meaningfully. But even of people who are lonely daily or all the time, only about one in five says they don't have what they need to live a meaningful life.

Disillusionment with the Church

So there is a connection between loneliness, meaningfulness, and church attendance. Is it as strong as it ought to be? More than one expert says no.

Van Opstal says, "The momentum of the culture of Christianity in the US is not toward biblical justice and risk taking. . . . But in that gap between *I don't have a paycheck* and *I have a mortgage* is a generation of people that's asking, 'How can I be a part of something that matters?'" She sees joining in the mission of the church as mattering more to people's sense of belonging than their having found a comforting church to go to on Sundays.

Hempell emphasizes a ministry that addresses cultural issues and how they connect to the Bible. Many leave, she says, because they "feel like the church is missing the point. Churches could get some really good feedback if they were willing to ask how people are feeling about the church's engagement."[9] So the curiosity extends not only to the individual but to how they see the world they live in.

Barna research has uncovered trends among Americans in identifying and practicing as Christians (see fig. 7.7). As loneliness has increased each generation, church attendance and identifying as Christian have dropped.[10] Barna found that self-reported weekly church attendance hovered between 40 and

Figure 7.7
Weekly Church Attendance: 1993–2020

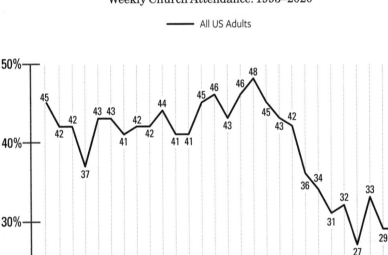

All US Adults

N = 103,603 US Adults | 1993–2020
https://www.barna.com/research/changing-state-of-the-church/

50 percent of the US adult population until about 2012. But it had already begun to fall. By 2020, far fewer US adults—29 percent—said they attend church weekly.

Similarly, the proportion of practicing Christians held steady from 2000 to 2009, but then there was a steep decline (see fig. 7.8). Today, a quarter (25%) of US adults are practicing Christians. The quarter of US adults who used to be practicing Christians but now aren't are about evenly split between no longer practicing Christianity and no longer identifying as Christians.[11]

The "nones" among younger generations are the subject of many conversations. But there are also many older adults who have also stopped identifying as Christians and going to church. In 2012, 53 percent of Elders said they attended church weekly. By 2020, only 37 percent did. In 2012, 44 percent of Boomers said they attended church weekly. By 2020, only 32 percent did.

While the research here doesn't indicate that there's a strong link between not being lonely and being a practicing Christian, perhaps there ought to be. That is, Christian leaders would love to see each person who starts coming to church feel enveloped, secure, and loved—right?

Hempell says that Barna has identified patterns among churchgoers and those who have stopped going. Those patterns can reveal some things about the way people perceive their churches, and it points to some reasons churches might be pushing people toward loneliness, rather than pulling them away from it.

With young people who identify as Christians, Hempell says, there are several variations on the way they connect to the church. "Some feel connected, and that's those where their family is reinforcing that connection." The faith in those households isn't purely cultural or habitual. "No, it's something we talk about at home, and we talk about at church."

"We have seen in the Association of Christian Schools International research we did that students who were most involved

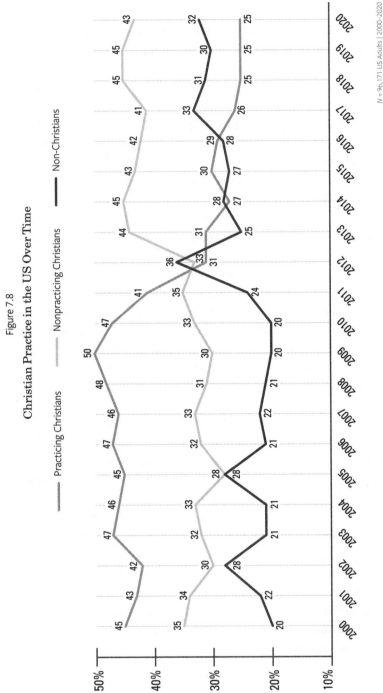

Figure 7.8
Christian Practice in the US Over Time

— Practicing Christians — Nonpracticing Christians — Non-Christians

N = 96,171 US Adults | 2000–2020
https://www.barna.com/research/changing-state-of-the-church/

and committed to Christian education were also most involved at their church and most involved in volunteering activities.[12] They were just all in," Hempell says. In other words, those young practicing Christians were deeply invested in their church and their faith. Young people with strong and resilient faith make up 10 percent of those with Christian backgrounds.

The second type of self-identified young Christian, Hempell says, is disconnected from the church. That group divides again into two. One group of those disconnected young Christians is "looking at the Christian faith and saying, 'I don't really believe it,' and they don't have a good outlet for wrestling with that skepticism. They're either afraid to bring it up, or they don't even trust that the church is going to have good answers, so they don't bother to ask. They just pursue their understanding, their worldview, through other sources." Hempell says those sources tend to be what's easily available online. This group often falls into the category of prodigals, which make up about 22 percent of young people with Christian backgrounds.

The other group of disconnected young Christians has "a desire to better understand their faith and to live out their faith very fully," Hempell says. "But they don't see that in the church, and so they're frustrated with the church." These are known as nomads, and they make up about 30 percent of young, self-identified Christians.[13] This group holds out an opportunity for the church to embrace orthodox faith and practice in a way that gives a place and a community for the many who feel disillusioned.

Sandra Van Opstal identifies the same problem, with a lack of trust in the church as a place to wrestle with faith. In particular, she says that "young people in their twenties are saying, 'We don't want to have to pick either our faith or a life of justice. We want to be able to do both, but we don't see any models of how that's done.'" Van Opstal knows of several self-organized groups of young people who are trying to understand these things, facilitating a conversation that their churches have ignored. Some of these are in Hempell's category of resilient disciples, but some are not.

Hempell says this group—the nomads—is the one most likely to talk about "decolonizing your faith" or "deconstructing your faith." They are seeking ways outside the church to reconcile what they think Christianity should be and what it is. Hempell also notes these people are saying, "'Look I grew up with this thing, and I think I believe it, but the church that I'm involved with—or the church that I see around me—isn't living out the principles that I think we're supposed to be living out. And so I'm either not sure of that faith or I'm not sure of this church.'" At this point, believing self-identified Christians often leave the church. They may still continue practicing their faith, but outside the community of the church.

Hempell thinks many churches miss the point that these disillusioned young Christians are making. "I think they're missing the reality of the gripe," she says. "This is genuine; they are reading the Scripture, and they don't quite understand how we're saying this one thing but we're doing this other thing."

These three ways of relating to the church while still considering yourself Christian are not, of course, within the power of leaders to control. But leaders can still anticipate and respond, protecting against loneliness by listening and seeking to be reliable.

Upended Hypothesis

Before the data came in, I had expected to see that practicing Christians were much less lonely than other groups. Given the socializing, the singing, the opportunity for meaningful work, the average age, and the marriage rate—as well as the sense of being a significant portion of our society—I'd hypothesized that the advantage would be significant. I had also guessed that some of those benefits against loneliness would dissipate when churches stopped meeting in order to slow the spread of COVID-19.

I was wrong on both counts.

From this kind of research, where we take a sort of snapshot of a situation, we don't know some important things about loneliness. There are several possible explanations, none of which we can prove or disprove without tracking individuals over time.

What if lonely people start to come to churches at a high enough rate to keep the rate of loneliness in the church the same as the US average? But do those people who came lonely become less and less lonely as they stay? What if churches are ministering to a group of people who are especially lonely, and they are keeping those people a lot less lonely than they would be without church? Those explanations would mean that churches are a force against loneliness.

But what if people become lonely in churches and leave, driving down the average rate of loneliness in the church? What if the different rates of attendance by older and younger Americans mean that churches minister to people already unlikely to be lonely? Or perhaps even before the pandemic Christians were shaken, grieved, or isolated in a way nonpracticing Christians weren't. Those explanations would mean that churches don't protect against loneliness.

I offer these examples to show that churches might not just be places where people experience loneliness at average rates. Right now, we don't know much about what kind of loneliness people on average experience over time in churches.

Although we don't have all the answers to these questions, there are some clear steps that leaders in the church can take to protect against loneliness, whatever is going on. They can go on with the good traditions of Christian meetings, like singing, rallying around the work laid out for us in the Bible, and resisting the temptation to dilute meaningfulness.

MYTH: Going to church makes people less lonely.

CORRECTION: Christians are generally as lonely as non-Christians.

THE TRUTH IN THE MYTH: During the pandemic, practicing Christians became much less lonely than other religious groups (nonpracticing Christians and non-Christians), indicating some previously hidden resilience to loneliness.

CONCLUSION: Something is working against the advantages practicing Christians have against loneliness: in-person time, singing, and more ought to give an obvious boost but don't. And something seems to be giving practicing Christians resilience against loneliness, even when their churches are not meeting in person.

8

PRIVACY

MYTH: When people are paying you attention, you won't feel lonely.

I first saw the movie *My Big Fat Greek Wedding* in a group that included at least one person named Nick. He had grown up just about where the movie was set, in the suburbs of Chicago. Nick and the other Greeks in the group were the first to laugh at every joke. They were so enthusiastic about it that they took a bunch of us out to Greektown the next night for dinner, insisted we dance the Sirtaki while we waited to be seated, then ordered for us off the menu. It was noisy and warm and fun. Just like the movie's introverted protagonist, I felt apart from but also embraced by all the clamor. I thought it would be great to be from such a big, boisterous family, even if it meant a pimple on my nose becoming an emergency for scores of cousins named Nicky. It seemed to me that privacy and a full life were at odds.

I wasn't alone in this idea. When asked in the winter of 2020 if they would choose a lack of privacy or loneliness, half (51%) of US adults said they would prefer to lack privacy, and a quarter (25%) said they'd prefer to be lonely. Another quarter (24%) said they didn't know.

However, Americans in general don't act as if we consider privacy a good exchange for feeling less lonely.

Privacy in America

If our desire for privacy can be measured by our willingness to share a bathroom, Americans' hunger for privacy, like loneliness, has been rising for decades. In US homes, there's now an average of one bathroom per person, up from one bathroom per two people fifty years ago.[1]

I live in an old row house whose floors are as effective as a baby monitor. I know at any point in time where my husband is. In fact, I'm pretty good at guessing where in their houses the neighbors are. No doubt they, too, know what I'm doing if they pay attention.

Even this is luxurious privacy compared to how many people on Earth live. Consider that 761 million people in the world don't have a bathroom in their home.[2] I once interviewed a family in the Philippines whose house was constructed of one-layered woven cane. The pleasant breeze came through, but so did the smells, conversations, and conflicts from their neighbors in a similar house four feet away.

Americans might have a high ratio of toilets per person, but our privacy is still less than many of us desire. Privacy is a hot-button issue in our time, partly because of the introduction of eavesdropping technology. Siri and Alexa are always ready to listen in. Neighbors' doorbell cameras record us on our strolls. Our phones can let people know where we are at any moment, assuming our phones are close by us.

Americans have both more and less privacy than we'd perhaps imagined a few decades ago.

Loneliness and Privacy

In the winter of 2020, only two in five (41%) of US adults said they had not lacked privacy in the past week. That is, three in five wanted more privacy. Fourteen percent said they always felt they lacked privacy, and another 22 percent said a lack of privacy was a daily struggle. Twenty-three percent lacked a sense of privacy weekly.

In the winter of 2020, before most households were socially isolating together, a lack of privacy, unpleasantly, rose with a feeling of loneliness (see fig. 8.1). In other words, someone invading your space is not the kind of friendship or company that solves disappointment in relationships. In *My Big Fat Greek Wedding*, the lack of privacy seems charming. In real life, the charm may not be there at all.

Confidants are one thing. Not having control over what you share or when—a lack of privacy—does not produce the kind of intimacy that staves off loneliness.

Of adults who had not been lonely in the past week in the winter of 2020, 61 percent said they had not lacked privacy, either. Adults who had felt lonely some but not all days of the previous week had a more even spread of privacy, with about half the rate (29%) saying they had had enough privacy. Those who were lonely on a daily basis saw a further shift toward a frequent lack of privacy, with 24 percent saying they had enough privacy and 18 percent saying they had never experienced enough privacy—more than twice the rate of those who had felt lonely during some but not all days of the week. Finally, of the group who said they constantly felt lonely, half (51%) also constantly lacked privacy. Only 12 percent said they had always felt lonely but never felt they needed more privacy.

This is not what I had expected. I'd asked about privacy thinking there might be a trade-off between loneliness and

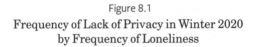

Figure 8.1
Frequency of Lack of Privacy in Winter 2020
by Frequency of Loneliness

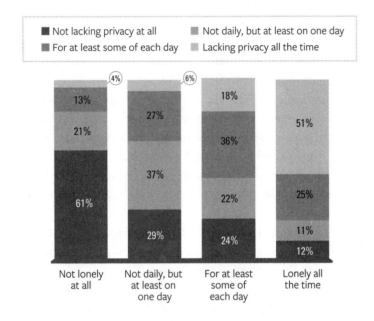

privacy. I guessed that having someone around who cared enough to ask too-personal questions and to be annoyingly ever-present might still alleviate loneliness. But I was wrong. It seems that for US adults, privacy is not the price we pay for satisfying relationships, even if half of us would choose to lack privacy (51%) rather than to feel lonely.

Loneliness and solitude—so often the chief pleasure of privacy—aren't closely related. People who are in a crowd may feel very lonesome. They may feel disconnected or emotionally unsafe. They may simply not have friendships with any of the people around them.

Being part of a crowd doesn't rule out belonging either. Some of us have experienced the unity and exhilaration of getting swept up with a crowd.[3]

Trade-offs of Privacy

I wonder, though: Could the desire for privacy have dual out-comes? The first is straightforward—that people need privacy in order not to feel lonely. The second is a little more complicated. What if we have such an insatiable appetite for privacy that we end up ruling out satisfying relationships? Maybe our taste for privacy grows as our skills for avoiding loneliness decline.

More and more Americans had started living on their own by the early 2000s. The number of one-person households in the United States peaked right before the 2020 pandemic.[4] When you live on your own, the home's level of cleanliness, its furniture arrangements, the way the towels are folded—all of these things are your own choices. When you live with someone else, you have to learn to work with someone else to make those choices or to deal with the conflicts they bring up.

It is good to keep in form for sharing life with someone else. In *The Four Loves*, C. S. Lewis says, "Our model is the Jesus, not only of Calvary, but of the workshop, the roads, the crowds, the clamorous demands and surly oppositions, the lack of all peace and privacy, the interruptions."[5]

This may sound very unappealing. Unselfishness often does. But it's also important to remember that, as with exercise and moderation in eating, you receive a return on the kind of responsiveness that cuts into your privacy. Leaders working against loneliness will keep this in mind, for others and for themselves: those who follow Jesus must also be willing to be interrupted and to lack privacy.

Privacy, too, has trade-offs. We can thrive in it. Or our discipline and even our character can suffer. Without a little shame, we might fail to keep standards that help us. Who doesn't tidy their house at least partly to avoid shame when someone else comes in? And many of us eat more chips or dessert than is good for us in the absence of another. Studies have shown—not with complete consistency—that there is a "watching eyes effect." If we're being "watched," even by a portrait on the wall or CCTV, we are more likely to do the right thing.[6]

The necessary balance of supervision and privacy, of being seen and invisibility, may vary across cultures and within a culture. But for all of us, privacy, when it goes too far, becomes social isolation. And for all of us, too little privacy can drive us a little crazy for lack of ability to process our thoughts in peace.

We need those watching eyes sometimes. They help us keep fit for a social life, including intimate relationships. But always being watched, paid attention to, or swept up in a crowd is no guarantee that we'll find the comfort and satisfaction we look for in relationships. We should start to examine our requirements for privacy more closely: What is our ideal? Is that ideal one that allows our lives to mesh with others' lives as intimacy requires?

MYTH: When people are paying you attention, you won't feel lonely.

CORRECTION: Among US adults, loneliness and too little privacy rise together.

THE TRUTH IN THE MYTH: When you engage with people and work on relationships that require sharing your space, you may end up with less privacy but more intimacy.

CONCLUSION: We need both privacy and company, for our own sakes and for the sake of our ability to function in society.

Part 3

PROTECTING AGAINST LONELINESS

We've seen who is lonely, along with the main reasons people are lonely. Now, how do people protect against loneliness? Is there a prescription for people by Enneagram type or star signs? Not really. Rather than aligning with typologies, resistance to loneliness seems instead to come from the nature of our relationships and the ways we think about them.

I'll highlight three elements that counter loneliness and seem to apply to just about everyone. These are *belonging*, *closeness*, and *expectations*. The list isn't exhaustive or verified by a separate study. Still, these three elements turn up over and over in research about loneliness and relationships, and good studies do show how these prevent loneliness.

A three-legged stool always has all three feet on the ground, but the seat might be at an inhospitable angle if the floor or legs are uneven. Think of belonging, closeness, and reasonable expectations as those three legs, holding up a surface that you can rest on and allowing your loneliness to subside. When our relationships have all three elements, they're more like the stool, which sits on the ground quietly and can support a lot of weight. But shorten or remove one of the legs, and the stool is no longer so reliable. Some of us could manage with two legs, vigilance, and some impressive abdominal and quadricep strength. But many of us would just have to stand back up again.

I should warn you: this combination of belonging, closeness, and reasonable expectations is not a formula that will keep someone from ever feeling lonely, even from being chronically lonely. Some people are simply prone to be lonely. Some loneliness is genetic, according to adoption and twin studies.[1] That means that someone's outward characteristics won't fully explain their risk of loneliness, and neither will their relationship quality. One study found that most people connect with others when they feel lonely and their loneliness subsides but that at least one in seven Americans is chronically lonely.[2]

In the Framingham Heart Study, people were much more likely to be lonely during one interview if they had been lonely during the previous one. Loneliness isn't like the seasonal flu, where everybody seems to get it at some point, then gets over it in a couple weeks. Loneliness won't necessarily respond quickly when people start to gain ground on satisfying relationships.[3] Satisfying, healthy relationships are worthwhile nevertheless. They are their own reward and the need to which loneliness points.

9

BELONGING

Relationships that produce belonging aren't rare. Many people find belonging in their families, which are ideal in many ways to provide strong, stable interpersonal relationships. While family can generate a lot of pain, many people also find that's where belonging comes easiest.

If belongingness is a fundamental need, we can expect people to be interested in forming new relationships (as we often are) and in developing some of those into long-term relationships (as we sometimes do).[1] Many of us also find belonging in the sort of relationships we form during elementary school recess or among colleagues. You might find belonging in any group you've had a home-cooked meal with. As you add branches to your family tree, you might find belonging there as well.

We all are prompted by loneliness to seek out belonging— and this is a good thing. In their article "The Need to Belong," Roy Baumeister and Mark Leary show that "it does not seem to make a great deal of difference what sort of relationship one has" so long as it fulfills the requirements of the need to belong.[2] In other words, you may not have a spouse or a mother, but friends can keep you from deep loneliness. Or you may not have friends, but your siblings may keep you from feeling lonely.

You might have close relationships with your mother and sister, but you will be happier, healthier, and less lonely if you also have a spouse, close friends, and dear colleagues.[3] Our need to belong is best met through a variety of relationship types. Exclusively depending on your family for belonging sets you up for loneliness.

This capacity to form and deepen new relationships is essential in a life in which we lose people. Baumeister and Leary's research shows that even the loss of a spouse doesn't prevent a person from forming a new life-giving bond with another spouse after some time has passed. A friend who moves away might always be dear, even if he or she isn't close enough to keep us from loneliness. But we can find relief from loneliness in new friends.[4]

Leaders protect against loneliness by creating and taking opportunities to see the whole selves of people under their authority or influence. Sanyin Siang says, "The way I define belonging is a feeling that your membership is accepted, recognized, and embraced. I think we all long for affiliation and membership."[5] But when we find that, "do we feel like we can bring our full self into a place and have that self be embraced?" Siang gives the example of working parents having to take care of their children during the many video calls in 2020. If leaders appreciate each person's whole self and all the roles they're playing, belongingness can take root.

How can leaders be ready for these deep, whole-self relationships? You can develop your own reliability, your own capacity to both give and receive help, your own time for being with buddies. For some leaders, this might sound impossible. But if you don't do it, you, too, will likely find yourself spreading loneliness from yourself to others.

Note that I'm not suggesting that you include people you don't like or can't trust in your inner circle. In being open to belonging yourself, with people you enjoy being with, you can make it possible for others. You are stopping the spread of loneliness.

We need to lean on others enough to stagger when they withdraw. But we also need to be strong enough that deep relationships don't have to be ultimate relationships. And we need to have multiple intimate relationships so that we can gain perspective and comfort when one of them is in trouble. In other words, our intimate relationships can help us help each other.

Security

One misperception of belongingness is that it requires a total match of lives. But for many people, that is out of reach. Security has to come from something other than a completely shared experience.

But insecurity, the topic of chapter 5, can also change our perception of belonging. Siang asserts, "We think that the default is people feeling that they belong. But I think the default is feeling like we're outsiders. If most people are feeling like they're outsiders, then I think we have to want to create a sense of belonging for ourselves." That requires a sense of security.

The classic case of insecurity is jealousy, which often alters how trustworthy we believe someone else is. Of course, jealousy does sometimes arise from untrustworthiness. But it can take on a life of its own, ruining relationships that could have been healthy. This sort of jealousy is a form of insecurity. Likewise, fear of missing out can be a form of jealousy and insecurity.

Siang says that when a group or team has a sense of belonging, "you get the sense that there is not jealousy. Jealousy is poison to a team. And when you have a group of people who are high performers, that competitive edge comes out. But when . . . each one of them feels like they belong, that competition with each other, that jealousy, drops out." She also notes that the members of the group become open to learning from each other and sharing of themselves. "We think about vulnerability as being able to share our worst self." Vulnerability also helps us to bring our very best to a group effort. Working for the good of the group, as well as openness, is a sign of belonging.

Siang says digital interactions don't have to be lower quality than in-person interaction, especially when there's high-quality listening, meaningful conversation, and some self-revelation going on. However, she says, "I'm discovering that most people aren't used to that." She suggests prompting people to develop those skills in digital interactions by using as many senses as they can incorporate and by deliberately going deeper, such as by naming each other's unique gifts or expressing gratitude for something that happened in your life.

Without emotional security, we have a difficult time finding belonging. Each relationship seems like a rotten floorboard. To others, a jealous person's accusations and need for reassurance (and often surveillance) are a strain. We can't get our security from someone else, and we can't stave off loneliness without it.

Brooke Hempell says Barna research has uncovered an imbalance of knowledge that she connects through insecurity to loneliness. This is the finding: we know all sorts of things about others who are anonymous to us, and yet many people do not feel really known by anyone. Speaking for the average respondent in the survey, Hempell says, "I am cognizant, very cognizant, of the unrest that's happening right now in Nigeria, and the hurricanes that have been hitting all of the Atlantic coast, and the wildfires in Portland and California. That's a lot. Also, I am less likely to say that I feel deeply cared for by those around me or that someone believes in me." It's an imbalance that can be very hard to handle. Many Americans experience it this way: "There's all this weighty stuff out here, but I don't have the emotional safety net that I need to navigate that."[6]

We need a "foundational sense of connectedness and love and nurture and security" to avoid being overwhelmed. Hempell says, "That connects to both the anxiety that we see and also the loneliness that people experience—not feeling deeply known."

Sandra Van Opstal maintains that Christians have a sense of security on several levels: "Christians find that sense of identity, that sense of worth, in who they believe they are in the mind of their Creator. There's intent in God's design for me even when I was in my mother's womb. Beyond that, there's a sense of belonging to a people and a community and a movement. . . . I'm supposed to demonstrate the love and justice of God in the way that I live in a community, in a neighborhood, with my finances. I think that that's intriguing. I think it's still intriguing to Christians of every generation."[7] These teachings about God's deliberate creation of each person can give people a sense of belonging that extends back before they were born. Van Opstal says that the purposeful work still to be done doesn't detract from that unshakeable belongingness.

That security in being loved from the moment God imagined us allows us to say, even if some people reject me, God loves me. People with this kind of security will nevertheless still feel pain, and may still need interventions, counseling, or relationship building. We need people. We also need to know that when people let us down, we are eternally safe and accepted.

Friendship's Importance to Loneliness

Matt Jenson sat across a desk from a new colleague and thought, *This guy and I will never be friends.* And for a while, they weren't—until Jenson needed to confide in someone and that colleague was the best choice. That confidence led to a friendship deep enough for the colleague's kids to call Jenson "uncle" and insist he is family.[8]

If belongingness is the near opposite of loneliness, friendship is often the most powerfully anti-loneliness form of belonging. Yes, even more than kinship. The evidence, especially as people grow older, is that chosen rather than inherited relationships are the ones that have most to do with loneliness.[9] (Marriage, discussed in chap. 4, seems to be in an intermediate category.[10] It is indeed powerful in preventing loneliness, but it does not replace friendship.)

The researchers analyzing the Framingham Heart Study in "Alone in the Crowd" found that loneliness spread more through our "optional social connections" than through social connections we have through kin—such as grandparents or siblings. In this study, if you remember, those kin and non-kin social connections are on a list of people study participants expected would be able to locate them in a few years. People we choose to become close to, rather than people we have natural intimacy with, have the biggest effect on loneliness.[11]

And who are those people we decide to become close to, those optional social connections? They are mainly significant others, colleagues, neighbors, and friends. Hopefully, the romance, neighborliness, and collegiality all come with friendship. Friendship can be an element of all sorts of relationships.

Research on American Friendships

A 2004 Gallup survey of close friendships outside of family revealed that Americans are generally satisfied with the number of close friends they have.[12] However, that number has gone down since 1990. According to Gallup, the average American has about nine close friends (technically, it's a mean of 8.6 friends—and I suppose some of us know who that fraction of a good friend is). In 2001, Americans had a mean of 9.5 close friends. In 1990, we had 9.9 close friends each. That's a drop of about one friend in the average person's life over the past thirty years. The median, possibly the best way to show what's normal, did not shift much, sitting at five close friends both in 1990 and in 2003.

Gallup found that 2 percent of Americans had no close friends. That was about 5.8 million people. To help picture how many of the people you see who might have no close friends at all, about the same proportion of people in the world have naturally red hair.[13]

So, what characteristics make a difference in how many friends a person has?

Age seems to. Again, flipping the narrative of the socially isolated retiree, people over sixty-five are likely to have more friends than younger Americans, with a mean of 12.5 close friends, compared to 8.7 among fifty- to sixty-four-year-olds and 7.0 among thirty- to forty-nine-year-olds. Young adults have the second-highest number of close friends, at 8.9. It's unclear if the difference is due to generational characteristics, cycles of accumulating and growing apart from close friends, or some other factor.

Even with the slight drop in Americans' number of close friends over the past few decades, only a little more than a quarter (27%) of Americans said they would like more close friends. Perhaps more surprising, only 18 percent said they'd like to be closer to the friends they have.

Some researchers have found that more friends means less loneliness. Others have found that even one friend can be enough and that, after a certain point, more friends do not make much of a difference to loneliness. How can we untangle these mixed messages about how many friends we should have?

Again, analysis of the Framingham Heart Study produced some of the best evidence here. The authors of "Alone in the

Crowd" looked at the number of friends and loneliness among the study participants over time. People who listed more friends in one round of the study were less likely to say they were lonely during the next. They also found that for each additional friend, people were lonely a little less often.[14]

You might not find an hour less of loneliness to be noticeable, but consider that if someone has one friend and you have nine (the average), they feel lonely over eight hours more each week than you do. Eight hours a week is noticeable.

The researchers found that when they looked at loneliness as a result of both the number of friends and the number of kin at the same time, an extra friend or two reduced loneliness, but the number of family members did not.[15]

In the Framingham Heart Study, lonely people named fewer friends. It worked the other way too: others were less likely to name them as friends. Clearly, there is a strong connection between the number of friends and loneliness. The authors concluded that "loneliness is both a cause and a consequence of becoming disconnected. These results suggest that our emotions and networks reinforce each other and create a rich-gets-richer cycle that benefits those with the most friends."[16] On the other hand, other studies have shown that after a certain point, more friends don't bring big benefits in terms of loneliness.[17] After all, some people do report loneliness when they have a lot of connections in their social network.

If each friend brought the same boost (and people were perfectly rational), we might start behaving in a way that would maximize friends. That would probably mean getting each relationship to a point where the friendship was official, then turning all our attention to the next friend to be made. Instead, we savor friendships and don't tend to seek them out as earnestly once we have a few. In practice, people generally value the quality over the quantity of friends.[18]

The authors of "The Need to Belong" concluded that people need one strong bond. But the real number of necessary close bonds seems to be more than one. Most people have the majority of their meaningful interactions with the same six people.[19] Beyond that minimum number of friends—whether one, six, or some other number—the researchers found evidence for diminishing returns on friendships.[20] That is, additional friends affect our lives less and less.

Many things work like this. Take, for example, thirst. If you've mown the lawn on a hot day, you might want a glass of water afterward. You will probably drink a lot fast, maybe three-quarters of the glass before you feel relief. You'll still be thirsty, but you no longer guzzle the water. Each sip makes you less thirsty, but with a smaller effect than those first big gulps.

While the question remains of how many friends a person needs, it looks like Americans might not be so badly off with the median of five close friends, or the mean of eight or more. And while I am concerned about the shrinking number of friends Americans have, it's the pattern rather than the current number that concerns me. If more and more people fail to build even one deep friendship, loneliness will spread faster.

Because of this, we need to value the early stages of friendships, including friends who are more buddies than soulmates. Buddies are in the pipeline to belonging. Not all will develop into deep friendships, but some will.

How Friendships Begin

Friendships generally begin with chance meetings. We meet people by accident in places where our characteristics make us likely to find people in common: neighborhoods with roughly the same family structure and income; colleges where people have a certain range of SAT scores; or, as in an experience of mine, lines to the bathroom at a conference that presupposes some shared values. From that point on, whether we get closer depends largely on randomly reencountering those people and then deliberately getting together. Those next encounters have a lot to do with convenience and our geographical range—how often our literal paths cross.[21]

These rules apply for the usual friendships, in which two people share a lot in common, from race to socioeconomic status.[22] But they can also apply to people who share some things in common—intelligence, for example—but not others, like ethnicity or first language.

This can help us think about how friendships can be prevented. First, we can fail to have chance encounters. Second, we can fail to interact during those chance encounters. Third, we can fail to deliberately meet up with people we've had chance encounters with.

The first way to prevent new friendship—not encountering others at all—is increasingly relevant. Japan's famous hikikomori, the young men who literally never leave their rooms, are a reality in American society as well, if on a much smaller scale.[23] For far more people, we risk having lives of such insularity that we have neighbors we've never met. Many people are good at creating a mental bubble, so that even when they are out walking around, they behave as if they were alone with their devices.

Sharon Hargrave points to initiatives Pepperdine University has taken to retrain young people who aren't open to chance meetings. The program has a simple message: Look up. Hargrave says the program encourages people "to walk through campus looking up at people. Smiling and engaging with other people seems like information that we should automatically know," but not everyone does.

This brings us to the second point. When you do find yourself in the same place at the same time as strangers, there's no surer way of getting them to interact with you than for you to interact with them. People push back against loneliness when they talk to strangers. And often strangers like having conversations.

Those strangers can be anyone, really, from colleagues whose names we never bothered to learn to a friendly looking person on the bus. Of course, this doesn't always work. I once had a neighbor literally run away when I introduced myself.

Sometimes, too, the missing pieces are social skills and a tolerance for initial awkwardness. And then secondary awkwardness, when you have to ask their names again. But if people persist, they find awkwardness fades and the names and details start to stick. Then there's potential for friendship.

Third, failing to get together with people we've met can prevent friendships from forming. The good news is that there is some built-in momentum to help friendships form from accidental encounters. We usually like people more the more we see them, for example.[24] So, say you've met a lot of people by accident, and you've spoken to many of them and you've run into them again. Which of these people is likely to become a true friend? Loneliness can't be solved, nor friendships formed, by being with just anyone; if you show up at a happy hour (a Washington, DC, specialty) or a church retreat, you may leave just as lonely and friendless, if not lonelier.[25]

Scott Frickenstein, founder of the coaching organization Leading by Design, learned through his twenty-five-year Air Force service to make friends quickly. He says, "I would look for mutual interest. So, on our very first assignment on active duty, there was a guy in the Bible study who happened to be a gonzo bike racer like I was. He also liked to hike and camp. His name was Alex. I just said, 'Alex, could we go for a ride or go for a hike?' And he was and still is the best friend I ever had."

Friendships are formed because of some shared interest or circumstance or just mutual admiration, but they are built on an increasing sense of belonging.[26] In *The Four Loves*, C. S. Lewis says, "The very condition of having Friends is that we should want something else besides Friends. . . . Friendship must be about something, even if it were only an enthusiasm for dominoes or white mice."[27] As with belonging, we do not find friendship in direct pursuit of friendship. But we may very well find it in pursuit of fun, or discovery, or fitness, or even a bathroom break.

How Friendship Changes Us

Friendship changes the way people think and act, expanding them in some ways. Many will have heard of the "bystander effect," where people may see someone else in distress (the murder of Kitty Genovese is the most common example—and the most gruesome) and reason that someone else will step in to help. But the bystander effect isn't at work in all groups. In groups of strangers, we may find the bystander effect at work when a problem persists due to lack of teamwork. But cohesive groups—that is, people who are friends or on their way to friendship—demonstrate the opposite. Group members, instead, are likely to help each other.[28]

When we feel loneliness, as we all do from time to time, those friends are people we can connect with, feel belonging and the good kind of distraction with, regain perspective with, and shed our loneliness for a while with. For most people this works well.

Matt Jenson certainly felt this. Single and wishing he wasn't, he wanted to have a confidant and many other things "that I think people in even halfway relationships don't even think about. Things like having someone whose job it is to be a regular witness of your life. Having someone to bounce things off of. Having someone to help with chores. And certainly intimacy." Not finding a romantic relationship for these things made Jenson invest in deep friendships. "My genuine need has made intimacy in friendship possible. I remember a time with a friend in grad school. We were both single. We would both start every semester on tip toes," looking at the incoming women to find "the one." "He and I would go on these long walks in the Scottish countryside. We were both really lonely, and I said, 'Can

I just give you a hug?' I hadn't hugged anyone for months."[29] Singleness pushed him to form rich friendships, ones he has kept, even after he eventually married.

Threats to Friendship

Lewis wrote extensively about friendship—in *The Four Loves* and elsewhere. Known in Greek as *philia*, the love that is friendship has enemies. He writes, "That outlook which values the collective above the individual necessarily disparages Friendship; it is a relation between men at their highest level of individuality. It withdraws men from collective 'togetherness' as surely as solitude itself could do; and more dangerously, for it withdraws them by two's and three's."[30] Lewis saw that the ideal of equal and similar relationships between all members of a group rules out true friendship. Leaders who are trying to protect against loneliness must remember not to prevent people from splitting off into small groups, even if it seems to be making the relationships in a group unequal.

I've seen several churches where conscientious folks avoid spending church time with those they know and like. There is kindness and virtue in this—it helps to prevent cliquishness—but there can be a problem with forcing friendship into a role of dirty secret. If friendship cannot coexist with hospitality, something has gone wrong. Churches and other institutions shouldn't endorse a model in which each person knows and likes every other person equally—or pretends to. As crusty as it may sound, there is some truth to the old saying, "A friend to all is a friend to none."

If you are trying to protect against loneliness, you have to accept the two-way nature of friendship. I once asked someone at my church to be a prayer partner because I liked her and wanted to know her better. We set up a time to meet, and she suggested I catch her up on my life first. When I was finished, she told me we could skip any prayer about her; she just wanted to encourage me. But instead of being encouraged, I was being put out of the friend zone and into the project zone. Our correspondence petered out quickly.

Another threat to friendship is as common now as it was in 1960, when *The Four Loves* was published, which is assuming any close relationship is romantic. Lewis writes, "It has actually become necessary in our time to rebut the theory that every firm and serious friendship is really homosexual."[31] Friendships can be hurt by the fear of being seen as a romantic couple or, alternatively, confusion about whether the strong feelings of a friendship are romantic love. But perhaps the biggest threat to friendship in our time is simply our damaged capacity for intimacy. Tim Keller writes, "Everyone says they want community and deep friendship. However, because it takes accountability and commitment we run the other way."[32]

Sharon Hargrave says she has seen intimacy damaged deeply by the label "toxic" being applied too broadly, leading to people cutting off anyone who doesn't meet their needs or otherwise do what they wish. "I've talked to people who have cut somebody out of their lives just because they wouldn't understand their holiday schedule," she says. These are people who "have gotten so angry that their adult children won't do Christmas morning with them that they cut off their relationship." Some relationships are toxic, she says, but "we [need to believe] that we can get through hard times in relationships, and they can be better and stronger because of those hard times."[33]

Friendships that don't stand the test of time or hardship don't stand the test of belongingness either. To protect against loneliness, leaders must learn to navigate disappointment in others and the conflicts that ensue. And they must learn how to help others do so too.

10

CLOSENESS

Stephanie Holmer had just finished her PhD in biochemistry and wanted to explore the world. She had been in that college town for six years. Like many of her friends and colleagues, Holmer was single. She was at the center of a big group of graduate students and other young adults planning camping trips, house parties, and after-church gatherings. But with her degree finally completed, she decided to take a long trip.

The flight miles must have been eye-popping. First she spent time in Kenya, then New Zealand. It was an amazing trip, one she still reflects on. But when she came back, her social life had nearly vanished. "I might have been starting with, like, 5 or 10 percent of what I had before grad school ended," Holmer says.[1]

She had to start over with a new roommate. Multiple close friends had moved away, leaving her with text threads. "People that I had anticipated would be there for me in that moment couldn't be there or weren't there. Either they'd started dating someone, and so they didn't have the time for a close friendship with me anymore, or they had actually left the area, and so just couldn't physically be present."

Her church had shifted its location to a theater. The previous church meeting place "had a very homey feeling to me," Holmer says. "I felt like when the service ended, I'd turn around and see a bunch of my friends, and we'd talk until they turned the lights off on us." The theater "felt like I was going to a Christian concert on Sunday morning. . . . I'd turn around and I'd just see everyone's backs heading out the door. So it was like, we went to a show and then we were leaving the show." Suddenly, Holmer realized she never got hugs. As she tried to rebuild belonging in church, she began to seek out churches where someone hugged her.

When people are lonely, and even when they're not, physical closeness matters. Loneliness tends to fade with physical closeness. One 2019 study refers to research showing that being physically close brings people emotionally close, a finding that goes back to 1950.[2] Being physically close means being close enough to hug, see each other face-to-face, and wave across the fence a couple times a day.

Hospitality

Hospitality is one form closeness can take. Broadly, hospitality means making someone welcome. For Christians, it's among the relatively few outright commands to the church: "Practice hospitality" in Romans 12, and "Do not forget to show hospitality to strangers" in Hebrews 13.

We've let hospitality go sideways a little. How can we welcome someone into a coffee shop or even on a walk when we're guests there too? Third spaces like that are important, but they are neutral ground, not our own homes. Inviting someone else to join you outside of your home is only the beginning of hospitality.

One of my favorite cookbook authors, Barbara Kafka, writes in the opening of her 1984 *Food for Friends*, "I'd found myself slipping into the trap of eating in restaurants, meeting friends for a drink or losing people altogether. I missed them and the leisurely evenings of food and conversation. People talk differently in restaurants, with less intimacy, less self-revelation. I can laugh more boisterously and tuck my feet up on my chair at home. Deep friendships thin in restaurants. When I was a girl, the rule of thumb was to meet new men for lunch or a drink out—to minimize the risk. That's fine for beginnings; but no guts no glory. So, for me, it has been back to entertaining at home."[3]

Hospitality may or may not require much preparation or food, but it does require self-revelation—that is, intimacy in at least one direction. Like Kafka points out, when you are relaxed at home, it means you can interact differently. COVID-19, of course, stopped most Americans from inviting people to their homes. But even before that, fewer people were having non-family members come over.

In a project Barna did with Lutheran Hour Ministries, *Households of Faith*, practicing Christians answered the question "Besides the people who live in your home, who else comes into your home on a regular basis (at least several times a month) and spends time with you or other household members?" The most common answer, selected by two in five (40%) respondents, was that no one came to their home on a regular basis. The next most common answer was a close friend (22%).[4] It's true that a majority of these households welcomed guests on a regular basis—but it still seems low.

The study also showed that generations of practicing Christians are more and more likely to have non-family members come to their homes. Fifty-four percent of practicing Christian Millennials, 43 percent of Gen X, 28 percent of Boomers, and 15 percent of Elders said that non-family members regularly came over to spend time with their family. The pattern for regular visits from family went more or less in the opposite direction

for practicing Christians, becoming more likely in older generations. Thirty-eight percent of Millennials, 31 percent of Gen X,
45 percent of Boomers, and 42 percent of Elders said they had
regular visits in their homes from family members. Do family
members crowd out friends as Americans age? Do older generations find that their families meet their social needs? Further
research may tell; for now, the answer is unclear.

A household or family might find it difficult to have people
over because of schedules or space. But they might find that
incorporating friends and extended family into their home life
keeps loneliness at bay. Certainly, it might for the invitees.

Physical Touch

Physical touch is another important form of closeness. Many
will know it as one of the five "love languages" described by
Gary Chapman, who says that while it's important for everyone,
some people find a hug "shouts love."[5]

Even if physical touch is more important to some people (or
they're just more comfortable with it), it has powerful effects
on all of us. Friendly touching—even something as simple as
a handshake—releases the "cuddle hormone" oxytocin. Oxytocin, like all hormones, is complex. It's what stimulates labor
contractions in women, so it doesn't always lead to warm, comfortable feelings. But it often helps people bond and feel trust
and contentment.[6]

Babies need to be held and cuddled. Adults can go longer
than babies without being touched or held, but going too long
without can lead to some of the same negative symptoms that
loneliness can produce.[7] If closeness can help us be less lonely,
can we get around forming relationships and just solve our
problems with a big dose of cuddle hormone? This question
has led to some weird behavior, including organized cuddling
of strangers and the rise of professional cuddlers.[8]

Oxytocin also exists in a nasal spray form, which is legitimately used in experiments on human behavior and suspiciously sold online to people who want the effects of social ease and emotional comfort.[9] (Please don't try to buy or use these; they are unregulated and don't necessarily have the ingredients or safety they advertise.)

And, of course, there are the people holding up signs for "free hugs."

For many, the idea of physical closeness leads quickly to the idea of sex. What if just having sex might make people feel less lonely? Even this has been studied. Multiple studies involved interviewing prostitutes about their relationships. Sex workers are a more reliable group than their clients for testing the theory that sex alone can make people less lonely. If sex alone could do it, you would expect prostitutes to feel a strong sense of belonging and to have very fleeting, if any, loneliness. Instead, they, like the rest of us, feel a need to invest in relationships outside work, and they don't seem to get a sense of belonging from their professional sex.[10] Sex alone doesn't cure their hunger for relationships.

One researcher at the Institute for Family Studies analyzed data about the link between loneliness and sex.[11] You might expect that people who hadn't had sex would be lonely. And they were; their loneliness was somewhere in the middle of the scale. But in 2020, they were no more lonely than people who had had sex with two, three, four, or more people. In fact, the least lonely group had had sex with exactly one person. Clearly, the main factor here is relationships, not sex per se.

Few readers, I expect, will be comfortable with the idea of cuddling strangers or sex for hire or sex with multiple partners as an experiment about loneliness. Nor am I encouraging any of these. These are symptoms of a culture where intimacy is inside out and where we constantly forget that even with consent and good intentions, relationships are more than the release of nice hormones.

I want to emphasize again that physical closeness isn't always sexual. Hugs from friends, sitting smushed up together with siblings to watch a movie, reading to kids who want to climb into your lap, holding babies—these are all parts of healthy, normal closeness, and they can be wonderful.

Physical intimacy without a lasting bond is no substitute for quality relationships or for belonging. But when there is belonging, people still need physical touch.

Neighborhoods

Closeness also comes in the form of neighborhoods. Living near someone gives them influence over your loneliness. Quite often, that's for the better. If our main goal was to minimize our loneliness, a good strategy would be to move into a neighborhood densely packed with friends.

In their study of the Framingham participants, the authors of "Alone in the Crowd" found that people were most influenced by people who lived very close to them: close friends within a mile and next-door neighbors came out as most influential.

When people whom a respondent felt close to were lonely, the respondent's loneliness increased as well. Some of that was due to proximity. A next-door neighbor feeling lonely had a bigger influence than a neighbor on the same block. A friend who lived within a mile had a bigger effect on loneliness than a friend who lived twenty-five miles away.[12]

Neighborhoods as well as neighbors matter. Ryan Frederick of SmartLiving 360 says that "this idea of place has been overlooked" but that the COVID-19 pandemic may have called much more attention to it.[13] A study of twin teenagers found that lonelier people perceived their neighborhoods to be worse in a couple of ways. First, they perceived their neighborhoods to be less cohesive; they thought that their neighbors wouldn't take action for the common good. Second, they saw their neighborhoods as messier, with more "litter, broken glass, rubbish in public places" and "groups of young people hanging out and causing trouble."[14]

So regardless of the objective state of their neighborhoods, lonely people perceive their neighborhoods to be less friendly and helpful and more trashy, with intimidating crowds of youngsters. Such perceptions can make us less willing to get out and participate, perpetuating cycles of loneliness. On the other hand, those who aren't lonely perceive fewer problems of cooperation in their neighborhoods, setting them up for friendly interactions with neighbors.

How our communities are designed can also affect whether we feel connected to friends and neighbors. Urban areas can lend themselves to this, as can any place that prioritizes human connection over cars. Unfortunately, many of our communities are built in a way that makes driving easier than neighborly conversation.

Frederick says that one of the key factors in fostering better interactions is to create an attractive environment. Another way is to make sure there's a place for neighbors to engage, usually by having something like a front porch, "an engaging front element to the house so that not all of the activity is in the back." Both Frederick and Andy Crouch mention a movement called "porching," which Joanna Taft of the Harrison Center for the Arts popularized in Indianapolis.[15] It's a deliberate attempt to get neighbors to share food and time on porches.

In addition, community planning can result in neighbors getting exercise together, walking or playing tennis, for example, or simply seeing each other as they drop children off at school or go about their business. Such efforts may very well put a more friendly face on neighborhoods and also help people feel that warm, safe sense of belonging and cooperation. We send signals about the sort of place something is with activities as well as architecture, Frederick says.

It's all fine and good to talk about neighborliness, but Americans' lives involve lots of moving. The average American moves more than eleven times, and for the average person, six of those are by age thirty.[16] How do you manage expectations of relationships when you don't have a very stable life?

Scott Frickenstein says that one technique military people like him often use is to be very quick to approach people for friendly activities.[17] If you think you like people, there's no reason to wait months or years to invite them over. Rather than make for a community as ephemeral as any one person's stint there, deliberate friendliness can change the sense of a place even with people coming and going frequently.

Another way to manage the frequency of moves in Americans' lives is to create better options for them from early adulthood on.

Frederick notes that many neighborhoods foster divisions not only by age but also by perspective, socioeconomic class, and more. "We've created these enclaves where we're not necessarily getting a diverse group of people in different ways." Making sure that lonelier groups, like young adults and singles, can live in a community that has nurturing characteristics means more single-family homes for rent, Frederick says, and may be addressed by cohousing or apartments with less individual and more shared space.

Those elements of closeness—hospitality, physical touch, and neighborliness—are most likely to happen if we initiate them. Leaders protect against loneliness by inviting people to their homes. Leaders protect against loneliness through touch (appropriate touch, of course). Leaders protect against loneliness by being good neighbors who give others every reason to expect cooperation, friendliness, and the look of a place that's cared for.

Stephanie Holmer did end up finding a church where people hugged her. She formed new local friendships and stayed in touch with the friends who had moved away. She also started dating her now-husband after her friends scattered. Currently an InterVarsity campus minister, Holmer reaches out to others in ways she had already started as a student.

11

EXPECTATIONS

Imagine you step on the scale after a year or so. You are surprised to see that you're much heavier than you used to be. You hadn't expected this; your sweatpants still fit comfortably. But it's a big enough increase in weight that you feel you've got to do something about it. You need a calorie deficit. There are a couple options to get there: by eating fewer calories than you burn or by burning more calories than you eat. That is, diet or exercise—or both.

If you think of loneliness like that extra weight, the solutions are similar. Loneliness, after all, is a difference. It's a difference between the relationships you want and the relationships you have. You should be able to ease loneliness either by making more of the relationships you have or by reducing the demands you put on your ideal relationships. Or both.

Either way, we protect ourselves from loneliness partly by adjusting our expectations. Reasonable expectations take into account constraints on our relationships—the limits on time and energy, competing obligations, multiple priorities, and more. Reasonable expectations incorporate grace—forgiving others because we also need and have received forgiveness; offering mercy and kindness, unasked; and not requiring others to run their lives on our terms or holding it against them when they don't.

Belonging and closeness boost our defenses against loneliness with higher-quality relationships. But by adjusting our expectations, we can hope for realistic interactions, reducing the demand side of relationships that can otherwise lead to loneliness.

I am not trying to make an ascetic of anyone. The ideal is not to reduce our demand for others until we do not require other people. That is not a Christian ideal. If it were possible, it would mean crushing our need for deep human relationships—a good, God-given part of our humanity.

C. S. Lewis condemns an attitude of trying not to need others when he writes in *The Four Loves*, "Since we do in reality need one another ('it is not good for man to be alone'), then the failure of this need to appear as Need-love in consciousness—in other words, the illusory feeling that it is good for us to be alone—is a bad spiritual symptom; just as lack of appetite is a bad medical symptom, because men do really need food."[1]

Our expectation should be that we need others and will feel lonely with too low-quality or too few relationships. Within that big expectation, though, we should consider how our expectations of ourselves and others can set us up for loneliness—or not.

Norms and Expectations

A few years ago, I was writing in a coffee shop while two women sat at the next table. I didn't pay them any attention until it became clear that the woman sitting diagonally from me had started to sniffle. She soon began to wipe her eyes. I tuned in to the conversation (I know, I know) in time for her to gesture with a now-wet napkin and say, "It's just . . . I didn't expect my life to be like this when I was thirty!"

Of course not.

I didn't tell her, since at the time I thought it might make things worse, that nobody expects their life to be like it is when they are thirty. Either what you had thought would happen (marriage and a couple kids, in her case) has not happened, or it did happen and it doesn't feel at all like you expected. The disappointment can be real, no matter how universal the unmet expectation.

Often we have a vision of what our lives should be like, and it depends on other people interacting with us in certain ways—proposing to us, accepting our proposal, giving us tenure, obeying us before we finish counting to ten. But we don't have control over others. We are setting ourselves up to be disappointed if we depend on someone else for fulfillment.

There's nothing wrong with being sad over an unexpected breakup or a missed promotion. We need goals that matter enough that we are disappointed when we don't accomplish them. We need relationships that are important enough to work hard for.

But quite often our expectations are based on assumptions rather than hopes. When we find ourselves or our coffee shop buddy dates leave us feeling lonely, we should ask why. The reasons we have or give might indicate we have expectations we should adjust or toss out.

Our expectations are often formed by norms. Norms, you won't be surprised to read, are what's normal. There is a norm in the United States of eating meat with dinner. There is a norm of wearing shoes in the car. Norms play a key role in behavior. We tend to become more normal—whether intentionally or not—when we know what the norms are.[2]

We don't necessarily get one consistent message about norms. Many of us find wildly divergent messages across groups—and we tend to choose the norms we see from people we want to be like. We learn which norm to follow from our reference group, the set of people we compare ourselves to. They are our counterparts, whether in reality or in our imagination. You likely compare yourself to your siblings or their spouses. You might compare yourself to neighbors, colleagues, or classmates from high school and college. You might even compare yourself to semiprofessional online influencers.

Norms can be great, terrible, or anything in between. Those reference groups and the norms you see in them might, for example, make you a better correspondent or a more honest person. This concept is behind some good initiatives, such as listing your neighbors' energy use statistics on your energy bill. If they are using less than you are, you will likely be more careful in the future. Norms might have a neutral influence, such as nudging you to put up a Christmas tree earlier or later.

But sometimes perceived norms can make you believe that everyone else is doing something that leads to heartbreak and that you should do that too (or that you are doomed to the same fate). Divorce can work this way,[3] as can obesity, smoking, and more. (The good news is that good things can be contagious too.)

Norms can lead to loneliness. You might have absorbed expectations of how many friends, how many visits, and what elements of a social life are normal and find that those standards make you miserable. Why? Because they lead you to expect a type or timing of interaction that isn't reasonable, and then, when others don't meet that expectation, you feel disappointed and rejected.

Imagine you start to believe that everyone goes out with friends every weekend and that you're a loser because you go out once a month. Imagine you believe that your adult children are letting you down because they don't bring the grandchildren over more often. You might not only feel rejected and disappointed but you might also try to get them to conform to your ideas of what's normal.

Consider what strong-arming a friend to go out to restaurants every weekend could do if his budget can't stretch that far, or what complaining about visits could do when a family is already sad that they have too few vacation days. They, too, might feel disappointed and rejected.

As we try to follow the norms of our reference groups, our ideas about what's normal change what's normal. Members conform to the expectations, if not the behaviors, of the group, then the range of expectations and behaviors gets narrower and sometimes shifts. This helps explain how groups take more extreme positions than individuals express on their own.[4] Unrealistic expectations based on norms that are badly suited to real life can lead to loneliness. And remember that loneliness is contagious, especially to people who are close.

Beware of norms, but use them. Consider offering comfort for things out of a person's control (being asked on dates) and encouragement for things in a person's control (calling a sibling). Use norms to others' advantage, such as by emphasizing the majority when the majority is doing something helpful. For example, most practicing Christians have friends come over on a regular basis. That statistic can make someone more likely to practice hospitality. Go ahead and cite it.

The word *algorithm* gets tossed around a lot and tends to imply mathematics beyond what most of us can grasp. In fact, an algorithm is like a flowchart of instructions. The difficult part is that they are usually written to be understood by machines. The algorithms I'm talking about here sort out what we see online. When we look at social media, we are seeing our friends and contacts through a filter designed to show us things that are in the interests of the platform's bottom line. That is, Facebook, Instagram, Snapchat, Twitter, and others do what they do primarily for their own benefit, not yours.

Your feed may present you with messages you don't like or messages you do like, but either way, an algorithm curates it to get you to interact more with the platform. When you look at social media feeds, you are not seeing what all your friends are saying; you are seeing what the algorithm thinks will make you click on something, anything.

In other words, to understand real norms and real lives don't use social media as a reference point. It's not designed for that. To understand norms about relationships, talk to people in person. Balance online activity with in-person activity. And be aware that you, like everyone else, live in a small, skewed world.

If you really want to know more about what people do and don't do, look at statistics from reliable organizations like Barna and the US Census Bureau. Statistics won't tell you everything about people's lives—in fact, they won't tell you much on their own—but they will tell you how normal something is.

Digital interactions form our expectations in another way too—by strengthening or weakening our social skills. Andy Crouch notes that when it comes to communicating through devices "this is a very deep underlying problem."[5] He goes on to explain, "I don't just need to be connected to other people; I need to be the kind of person who, given a connection, can make something of it. It turns out it's actually quite difficult to make something of it." Communication may be easy, but relationships still take effort and practice. "It's difficult to have a conversation. It's even more difficult to sustain a relationship through conflict," Crouch adds.

Digital natives, as well as people who haven't kept in form for new friendships, may find that—especially without practice—"if I haven't built up even some just very rudimentary skills on the way to that conversation, then the kind of conversation I'm able to have is quite thin." You might have had conversations like this, where you never seemed to get any traction. Crouch says, "One of the many things you hear a lot is 'we're more connected than ever before but more lonely than ever before,' and I think that's because the persons who are on each side of the connection have had less chances to develop personhood." Under those circumstances, "who cares that we're connected, if we have nothing to give each other?"

Context Differences

We are also sorted into little groups by real life, and the expectations within those groups might be very different. They can help us deal with some hardships as well.

For example, where you live, do white-collar workers generally have suit jackets at the ready? Are White people a minority? Do daily walks take you past grand marble buildings? Those things are true in Washington, DC. If I took what I see around me as the norm everywhere, I would have a very skewed idea of life in California or Montana.

Or take military life. A military family can expect to move a lot. They might have many friendships that they formed during a couple years when they lived close to their friend and then carried on long-distance for decades. This would be hard on most people; it is also hard on many military families. But as a group, they expect frequent moves, and the group understands the need for quickly formed friendships. In this case, expecting short periods in any one place prepares people to behave in ways that can prevent their own and others' loneliness.

Narrowing the difference between our expected and real relationships pushes loneliness away. We can change what we expect of relationships in a way that preserves them. We can expect fewer text messages from people with poor internet connections. We can expect a hiatus on camping trips with friends who are new parents. We can expect the rate of new friendships to slow when we finish our education. How do we know how to adjust?

Again—I can hardly say this enough—it's important to have high-quality (ideally in-person) interactions in which you shoot for a high ratio of listening to talking. Yes, even with people you've known since birth. You will understand their context not by talking to them but by listening to them. Become curious about their lives.

Expectations also come out of our beliefs about who is responsible for what. When we make others responsible for our own feelings or relationships, we will have trouble keeping those relationships when, inevitably, we get hurt. We might always expect the other person in our relationships to bring about the outcome we want. But Sharon Hargrave says, "What we tend to do is we blame it on the other person, but we need to start thinking about, *What am I doing that's possibly causing damage or causing problems in this relationship?*" Once we've asked that question, we can start learning about what we can change and what we can expect of ourselves and others. Then, Hargrave says, "I open the door up for more healing and more intimacy and more closeness to happen in the relationship."[6]

A Note on Mental Illness and Loneliness

Mental illness, in its many degrees and forms, is usually accompanied by loneliness. Loneliness can greatly increase our suffering. Does loneliness cause mental illness, or does mental illness cause loneliness? Or do they each contribute to the other? There does seem to be a terrible cycle of loneliness, mental illness, socially rejected behavior, and isolation.

Good and stable relationships protect people from many forms of mental illness.[7] Isolated people are more likely to have "behavioral pathologies, ranging from eating disorders to suicide."[8] So bad or missing relationships with, for example, a parent might kick off loneliness, which might lead to mental illness. One study found that while depression and loneliness often go together, depression doesn't by itself cause loneliness.[9]

Another study, focusing on PTSD (post-traumatic stress disorder) among veterans, found that loneliness was the most direct antecedent of mental illness and social dysfunction among people who were reacting to stress from combat.[10] Veterans who felt they belonged seemed far better able to process combat without suffering from PTSD.

Experts in the need to belong point out that many of the things people go to counselors for—"anxiety, depression, grief, loneliness, relationship problems"—can be explained by their reactions to the threats they see to their bonds with others.[11] They are trying to protect their relationships.

My point is not that loneliness is the root of all mental illness. But it's a main cause of suffering and weakens the resilience we need to be emotionally healthy. This book is no substitute for therapy. But counseling and other measures may be less effective if those who are most connected to people with mental illnesses are unwilling to be close to them. Nurturing relationships of belonging could help save lives.

Solutions and the Fine Print

There's no surefire way to end loneliness. The solution is not true love; it's not a one-night stand. It's not virtue or closeness to God or wealth or beauty. It's not logging into or quitting social media. In fact, even if you practice everything in this book, you and those you care for will almost certainly feel lonely again.

Other solutions sound far more promising at first. For example, scientists are trying to develop a loneliness pill. The pill, which delivers the hormone pregnenolone,[12] targets some of the distortions loneliness can bring. Specifically, it tries to clear away the effect of loneliness that can make us perceive constant rejection or emotional threats—and avoid getting close to people.

If such a pill were safe and effective, it would be wonderful. It could throw a wrench in a vicious cycle. But, as with the medications that have made such a difference to people suffering from anxiety and depression, people will still have work to do and insights to gain. The pill would remove barriers lonely people have that prevent new or close relationships, but the pill would not be a substitute for relationships.

Another solution is providing outlets for socializing where people already have to go. In Europe, some supermarkets have "chatty checkouts" for people who would like to talk while in line to check out.[13] Having a captive but willing audience might help lonely people and socially isolated people. They can anticipate and count on that conversation.

What if you could have a conversation partner whom you could confide in—would that solve loneliness? Already, multiple robots are designed to help lonely people—and they do.[14] "Carebots" help disabled people, while others are designed to be like pets, still others like human companions. They can also, like the loneliness pill, help people overcome some of the barriers to real relationships. For example, they might revive some social skills in people who have been homebound for a long time. This isn't *Star Wars*; few Americans have robot companions at this point, and those who do tend to be older.

Another very popular way of trying to assuage loneliness is getting a pet. Pets, particularly dogs, have many benefits; however, as an animal lover it pains me to have to convey that there isn't clear evidence that having a pet effectively makes someone less lonely.[15] By contrast, *belongingness* is what addresses loneliness in the long run. Companionship may be something we appreciate in a wide range of beings, but only other humans meet our needs for belonging and intimacy.

Loneliness still crops up, even when people invest in relationships that offer belonging and closeness and come with reasonable expectations. For now, it's part of being human to feel from time to time that we're out in the cold, looking in. And that's not wrong. Again, the problem with loneliness is what it signifies about relationships, and sometimes what underlies loneliness is that we never feel completely united to others.

12

BREAKING THE CYCLE

Even if you don't love nature documentaries, you might have seen an image of emperor penguins huddling together at the South Pole. The penguins are a community with one really big problem: their environment. As temperatures fall at night, the penguins form what looks like a blob from overhead. Penguins keep shuffling up, finding a little space, and wedging themselves in, putting their faces down as they do so. The scrum of penguins keeps them very warm—even seventy degrees warm—when warmth can mean life or death.[1]

They also keep warm by shuffling: the penguins in the warm center get rotated out, while the penguins with ice on their rumps get rotated in. Everybody gets a turn. As a group, they can make it through the winter nights.

People, of course, are dealing with much more complexity and variety than penguins. But we could be communities that deal with the loneliness that affects us all. I'm not suggesting we humans rotate so that some of us are lonely and others are not on an occasional basis. But we can cooperate as a community with the understanding that we are all vulnerable to the same problem and all in need of others. Even if one or two or five relationships keep loneliness at bay for someone, it takes a community to support those relationships. Leaders play an important role in creating a culture that incubates relationships.

Below are suggestions from leaders who are protecting against loneliness. Some suggestions might work better than others in creating a community that is an incubator for belonging, closeness, and reasonable expectations, but these are all good things to do.

Leading by Example

The way we perceive loneliness—our own and others'—greatly affects how we address it. In fact, this book is designed to help readers perceive loneliness more accurately and sympathetically. Knowing that loneliness is disappointment in relationships, or insufficient intimacy, and not simply social isolation or solitude may shape how leaders interact with lonely people.

And what about those lonely people? It's important that leaders learn to double-check their stereotypes. They should ignore whether someone gets a senior discount or seems a bit of an underdog—those are not distinctions between lonely and not lonely Americans.

I have a high regard for the intuitions that come from experience, but without feedback and lots of practice, our intuitions are all too often stereotypes. That is, they aren't dependable, and they probably get in the way of relationships. In part 2 of the book, you read about how many of our stereotypes of lonely people are false. Instead, if you must have rules of thumb, look for groups that are disabled or bereaved. Pay special attention to groups that already have it tough or have had it tough for generations. In particular, look for people going through transitions in their identities and relationships.

But still, beware of applying these rules of thumb to each individual. Did that particular person get lonelier during the

COVID-19 pandemic, despite national trends? Why is another person lonely when they have none of the risk factors for loneliness? Answers to those questions can come only from real knowledge of those people. And that will mean interacting with them rather than with statistics.

People look to leaders for solutions. This will come as no surprise. As leaders protect against loneliness, there are some things they can do as individuals. (Most things in the following sections are things a culture or a community must participate in.)

Many people want fast solutions to loneliness: for a spouse to be lectured so that he or she will become nurturing, for a demon of loneliness to be prayed away, for a certain type of relationship to form so that someone will not feel lonely anymore. In the face of this, leaders need to be honest about quick fixes. Loneliness is unlikely to disappear more quickly than a friendship takes to mature, or more easily than the last five pounds of extra weight.

In addition, you need to be present and responsive. Caelene Peake says she looked for "a pastoral ministry that isn't afraid to approach all the suffering head-on and go to those places of pain with you. And cry with you and weep with you and not brush it all off."[2] While not everyone will want to cry, they will need someone who does better than brush it off.

Understand also that people in your sphere of influence may be holding or spreading harmful ideas about loneliness—that it is sinful, that it indicates lack of spiritual growth, that once you meet the love of your life, loneliness will melt away. You don't have to teach these ideas for them to spread, but you very likely have to contradict them for them to stop spreading.

Peake remembers hearing her loneliness described as a demon, as generational sin, or as nothing at all. She was told, "Honey, Jesus will meet all your needs." The leaders and others who talked with her about loneliness tended to see her problems as otherworldly, missing the fact that they were caused by low-quality relationships as well as her family's need for the gospel and her need for sleep and clean laundry.

Fostering Belonging as a Leader

You've probably heard that it's lonely at the top. In fact, people with power are quite often people who have a sense of belonging, and they are less likely to be lonely than people who feel powerless.[3] People with power are lonelier only under certain conditions. Those include having responsibility for meaningful and negative outcomes, like laying off employees or whistleblowing.

Military leaders sometimes meet those conditions. Because their role is around the clock, they don't have subordinates who can be buddies in off hours. Scott Frickenstein was a wing commander, one of five colonels on a military base, and he quickly recognized that he and the other colonels' families were likely to feel isolated if they didn't act. So, he says, "we talked to our boss and said, 'Hey, can we get a monthly potluck going? We'll host the first one.' And every month we have a potluck amongst the senior officers." He believes it really helped to have some people he could be casual with on a regular basis and to "combat the loneliness of command."[4]

Leaders who are protecting against loneliness may find themselves in a similar position. Banding together with colleagues or other people you can be open with may protect against your own loneliness.

Even though he couldn't create a sense of belonging among people on the military base by becoming buddies with them, Frickenstein says, he could still do a lot to protect against loneliness. He notes how Philippians 2 describes Jesus: "He made himself nothing by taking the very nature of a servant, being made in human likeness. . . . He did not just remain where he was," Frickenstein says. "He made a huge effort to enable us to feel a sense of belonging. Jesus was out and about; he chose twelve to be with him. He didn't say, 'Hey, guys, I'm gonna give you a briefing once a week on PowerPoint, and just try to keep up with me.' In between times, he was with them.

"And so, as a senior officer, I would routinely go to the workplaces of my people. I would go to the back shops, to the people who are working on electrical stuff or the roads, the people who are doing customer service at our library or at our bowling center—just being out and about with people. I scheduled time with each unit to be at their physical training, whether it was flag football with the firemen or basketball with the communication squad."

That time with people is what gave Frickenstein an opportunity to find out what mattered to his people and what was going on in their lives. And he made a point to follow up with people if he heard they had lost a family member or something similar.

Leadership and Devices

When it comes to devices, leadership means not allowing devices to become our masters. Technology, Andy Crouch says, "is about effortless power." We adopt new devices and applications because "they reduce the effort required to feel like I'm making a difference."[5] But it's easy to let devices and apps hinder in-person relationships, as well as the solitude that can be an important reset.

Crouch has made it his practice not to carry his cell phone and other devices with him all the time. He says, "I have this weekly rhythm as well of getting rid of it about one hour a day, one day a week, and one week a year." It's a matter of discipline for him, but it's also a family approach—Crouch co-authored *My Tech-Wise Life: Growing Up and Making Choices in a World of Devices* with his daughter, Amy Crouch. Amy, when advising about using devices, says not to go to sleep with your phone. "Let your phone go to sleep before you do, and get up before your phone does. Keep your phone out of your bedroom."

But just as important, Andy says, devices often compete with "a really durable witness from the Christian tradition that solitude, silence, and fasting are fundamental disciplines. The tradition . . . returns to these three." He says our devices "guarantee that you never get at least the first two." As for fasting, "if you think of fasting not just at the level of food but at the level of appetite or reward," sort of like the dopamine hit you get from food or some online interactions, "then our phones are fully in the category of things that do not allow you to fast."

Crouch has implemented safeguards to make sure he doesn't return from his time away from email to have to make up for it. He also took a break from Twitter in order to finish his most recent book. "I changed my Twitter name to 'Andy Crouch is Away at the Moment,' and I definitely felt a twinge of FOMO when I made that decision, even though I knew I just had to do it for my serenity and creativity." He says it's been humbling to realize that he didn't need Twitter for news after all. "All the important things I found out about other ways. . . . What I gain from detaching myself from devices and the need for significance—which is really the underlying thing—is freedom."

Seeking Justice . . . and Community

Working toward justice can protect against loneliness in two ways. First, justice affects people who feel they don't belong and can't trust others. Its aim is to bring about their flourishing and to break down the things that interrupt belonging. Second, as Sandra Van Opstal observes, people often find that pursuing justice brings belonging to the pursuers.[6] That said, most people do not automatically find the stamina or resilience for working for justice.

In her Chicago neighborhood, Van Opstal has seen waves of Christians move in who are almost always "folks of privilege, regardless of their race, that relocated into communities of color that are systemically under-resourced. They don't last long before they're in therapy because they can't take the weight of injustice that they see." She says it's not moral strength that makes the difference, but community.

And there is a lot to learn from communities without privilege. Van Opstal says there's a difference between romanticizing poverty and seeing rightly that there is enormous resilience there. From that can come healing for all kinds of people. "I've seen it happen as people move into our neighborhood. The ones who connect to a small group of older Puerto Rican ladies or the Black praying mamas on Saturday—they actually make it. The ones who stay with their relocated, college-educated displacement group—they typically don't make it. They'll end up moving out." The key is finding a community to learn resilience from.

Still, Van Opstal says, "I would hate to communicate to people if you just live a life that is meaningful and you chase justice, then you will never feel confusion or loneliness again. . . . You actually could feel more of it." We need others, even when they don't solve our loneliness, to guide us through it.

Parenting Lonely Children and Adults

Leadership may not mean speaking at a podium or having ten thousand online followers. It may mean parenting. Because of the patterns of loneliness across generations, Boomers and Gen Xers may find themselves watching their adult and teenaged children struggle with loneliness.

If you know any new parents, you know their obsession: sleep. There are multiple strategies for getting babies to sleep, but sooner or later most parents find they have to let their child cry. The stronger the baby's will, the more excruciating it will be. I thought I was being kind to my baby by comforting him and putting him to sleep in my arms each time he woke in the night. For a while, that meant two wakeups a night. Then three. In the course of a week, it degenerated to every two hours, then every hour, then on the crucial night, every thirty minutes. At this point, I could barely tell a toothbrush from a shoe, but I was finally open to my husband's suggestion of letting the baby cry. It worked. Not right away, but after a few nights. Babies need skills to fall asleep, even if it just means sucking their thumb or wriggling into a better position. And I had to back away for my child to develop those skills.

Watching your child in pain can be awful when you know exactly what needs to happen for them to stop hurting and start healing. But just as you can't make a baby sleep, you can't make anyone form or conduct fulfilling relationships.

Sharon Hargrave sees that young people generally need less instruction and attention from their parents. She sees many parents who "want to hear from their children every day—even at college. A lot of parents, if a child doesn't send a text back immediately, will get concerned or upset or frustrated."[7] But parents who solve their children's problems so that their children will never feel bad are preventing them from developing key self-regulation skills.

Hargrave sees some loneliness among young adults as a result of that overprotective and overdemanding parenting. The price of raising children not to feel pain or rejection is loneliness. Protecting against loneliness requires that we know how to deal with the low and uncertain moments in relationships. It pushes us to make relationships authentic and intimate. Parents cannot do that for their children.

What can be done? As parents, "we need to be a supportive presence in their life without being a demanding presence," Hargrave says. "A helpful parent is a listening parent." Listening, supporting, and waiting may seem unnecessary and even nerve-wracking, but these, too, are skills that protect against loneliness. For example, if your child has told you how soon they'll respond to emails or text messages, you will feel less anxious or rejected if you simply take it at face value. If you don't know when they'll respond, why not ask?

Hargrave says that if parents aren't certain by college whether their children can solve problems, then it's time to let them go through the difficult process. It certainly doesn't mean abandoning them. "Pointing out a strength to them is the better way" to help them solve problems, rather than trying to tell them exactly what to do, or to solve their problems for them, Hargrave says. Keep in mind that your children have other resources, from school counselors to Google, to go to for advice. Their need for you is not always of the same nature.

And they often do need you. The *Households of Faith* report shows that teenagers have a special relationship with their mothers. Teenagers who are practicing Christians say that, of anyone in or outside their households, mothers are the ones they most frequently eat meals with (85%) and talk about God with (70%). They go most often to mothers for advice (78%), encouragement (75%), sympathy (72%), prayer (63%), answers to questions that bother them (78%), and answers to questions about faith (72%) (see fig. 12.1).[8]

Fathers were seldom far behind in these nurturing roles.[9] But they play a not-celebrated-enough role in developing self-control and other emotional skills in their children. Fathers' and mothers' skill sets overlap, just as there is a good deal of overlap in the reasons their children come to them. But they also have some distinct strengths, and both sets of distinct strengths can protect against loneliness.

Teenagers, as well as younger children, need family time. One study of teenagers during the pandemic found that most of them were doing better than expected. The researchers credited this to more family time, more sleep, and possibly more balanced social media use.[10]

These are key insights, and they should help people pause before blaming young people's problems on digital communication. Teens don't need only limited time on social media.

Figure 12.1

Teens' One-on-One Time
with Various Household Members

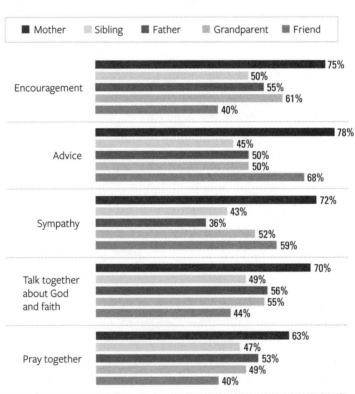

N = 448 US practicing Christian teens. Respondents were shown only relationship types they live with or those who regularly visit them in their home.

Consider what remains when you take away social media: does that person have high-quality time with family? Sometimes it's a simple either-or choice between family time and cell phone time. But one study also found a link between loneliness and poor family communication. If a family's communication was low-quality—for example, if teens felt no one was listening to them—they didn't experience a big difference between family time and digital communication.[11] That's like drinking only soda and finding Red Bull to be fairly neutral, rather than drinking fresh fruit juice and water and finding Red Bull to be overpowering.

So parents who wants to help a child be less lonely can first work on the way they conduct conversations. Are you, the parent, listening responsively? Even if you know your child so well you can guess his or her opinion, are you still asking? Are you letting misunderstandings fester, or are you trying to straighten them out? Even when enjoying each other's company might seem far in the past (or future), you can seek out reasons to admire your child and appreciate his or her personality.

A parent's role in protecting against loneliness is important. Your teenagers need you, and so do adult children. However, they don't need you to need them to need you. Parents will help protect against loneliness in their family by having multiple close, healthy relationships in which they find belonging.

Parents also can create a household culture that protects against loneliness more broadly. While leaders might try to, for example, promote hospitality and neighborliness among a large group, no leaders have a more influential role in making these things a normal part of life than parents do.

Dealing with Bouts of Loneliness

Dealing with loneliness, Hargrave says, has a few components. First, we must understand loneliness to be a gauge. Occasionally it's normal for the gauge to warn us. "If I'm driving and I see the gauge in my car going toward E," she says, it's time to look for a gas station. Loneliness shows us it's time to think about relationships.

In addition to needing social skills and context to manage loneliness, people need coping mechanisms. For example, if individuals find out via social media that they weren't invited to an event, they need to deal with their negative emotions with good rather than harmful coping mechanisms. And that takes preparation. In the moment, "the amygdala gets involved. I might do things that are destructive. I might get critical of my friends" or, alternatively, reach out to someone else, Hargrave says. The key is not only identifying what you're feeling when you feel lonely but also identifying how to approach it.

Hargrave reports that you can respond to loneliness by looking at old photos and remembering happy times. You can listen to music that makes you feel good. And then, with emotions no longer in a downward spiral, you can start addressing your loneliness. There is a wrong way to deal with it, she says, and that's assuming that your problem of loneliness should be solved by someone else.

Such approaches can be taught, because they are skills we can all develop. Leaders who are concerned about their own loneliness might work with a counselor; leaders who are concerned about a group's loneliness might take Hargrave's team's approach and implement a strategy that targets the most common problems on the way to satisfying relationships.

Strategies for Leaders

Identify and Normalize Loneliness

Hargrave says one of her team's strategies is to "help people understand that loneliness is a normal feeling, not a feeling that they're just experiencing themselves." Since we can assume everyone is going to have times of loneliness, "what we're doing is working with them to say, 'You're having this feeling of loneliness. It's telling you something. It's telling you to make a change.'"

In addition, people ministering to young people should normalize loneliness. Hargrave says that while pastors and youth group leaders typically concentrate on empathy and listening, they should also reveal things about themselves. "A lot of times, young people will look at a pastor or youth leader and see them on a pedestal, as a person who has no problems," Hargrave says. When a young person finds their own life different from perceptions about their leaders' lives, "it can increase their own sense of loneliness, because they believe their experience is different from anybody else's—and it's truly not."

This doesn't have to compete with sharing the joy of Christ, Hargrave says. "Pastors and youth leaders certainly want to communicate about the relationship with Christ and the support that we get from being Christians, but they have to counterbalance that with how that works in our lives." Sometimes the feelings of closeness aren't there—what can leaders teach about that?

Brook Hempell agrees. One of the biggest barriers to young people participating fully in the church is that "they feel like the church feels like they have to have it all together."[12] Normalizing seeking help and talking about loneliness can help dispel this myth.

Be Curious

Hempell goes on to explain that appealing to curiosity is the number-one approach for ministry to young adults. "That's how people know that they are deeply loved and that someone wants to deeply know them," she says. But it's not only for young adults; curiosity is a posture that allows all of us to understand and enjoy others.

Hempell says curiosity is not only asking questions but also "really wanting to get to know them individually. To really want to press past those nice things that we say and do, to 'Who are you really and what questions are you wrestling with?'" When you find out someone is lonely, talk through it. Why? What's going on in their lives?

Van Opstal says we can foster belonging by talking about rather than tiptoeing around emotions. Leaders "need to be in the business of just asking questions and receiving the response," she says. "There is a student in my life, and every time I see her, she looks sad and withdrawn. Lonely." Van Opstal asked her about it: "Hey, you seem quiet or sad or down. I'm not sure what it is. What is it? Tell me what you're feeling." The student responded that she was just tired. Sometimes there's more a person wants to talk about, if asked.

She was also in touch with "a young Black man who was having a lot of anger around what's happening around law enforcement. He was feeling very hopeless. Very angry. Very scared. Lots of fear about just going outside." Van Opstal saw his social media posts and got in touch directly. "Hey, I see you. I can tell that you're angry. And you know, I'm angry too. I just wanted to let you know I'm here." An older man who was in a mentor position had not approached this young man with curiosity. He had tried to change the young man first rather than listen, and it had not gone well. Van Opstal says to concentrate on "acknowledging and observing the behavior or the feelings that you see without judgment."

Stephanie Holmer says churches sometimes have too many people who are complacent about new people or people who don't share their culture. "Sometimes they just really lack that curiosity. And since they've never had to experience extreme hospitality or to try to integrate themselves into a totally different community, they lack some of the skills . . . to realize that the stranger in their church or town is a real gift for them."[13]

Foster Quality Time

One study on loneliness throughout life found that, despite the notion that loneliness can be addressed by meeting and reconnecting with people, so far there's no reason to believe such interventions do much good.[14] In other words, you will not solve loneliness in your community with a coffee or happy hour. You might not solve it with any formal program, in fact.

Programs to help lonely people are not generally reliable for ending loneliness. They may work for some individuals, and they may work in conjunction with other changes, but they simply can't be counted on. However, there are some important caveats. First, if people are for some reason unable to interact with others, interactions will often be a relief. There's nothing wrong with giving people a chance to mill around and meet each other, even if they stay lonely. Second, relationship building can happen in the times and spaces outside a program. It can happen when people are discussing the topic at hand as well as their personal lives, but it can't happen if they aren't interacting at all. It's important that a program's agenda not crowd out relationship building.

Hargrave says that before and during the pandemic, as churches and organizations tried to make video calls replace in-person time, she has been "really amazed that there is an overwhelming response that we keep getting back." People are telling the Boone Center for the Family, "I wish there had been more time for small groups . . . more time we could have talked to each other." Having unstructured social time is important; so is having something useful to do.

Matt Jenson advises people to "just do anything" at their churches to get involved. He at one point started counting the offering with an older widow at his church, and they formed a cross-generational friendship. "I don't know how many times we missed the whole sermon," sharing about their lives, disappointments, and loneliness.[15] They became friends just because they were willing to count the offering.

The best church programs will go beyond having attendees sit in a circle or in rows; such programs, I suspect, turn attendees into audiences. I believe the best programs will use the time people have already committed to a program for cooperative, interactive work that involves minimal awkwardness.

What if you discovered that people at your church bond more while making materials for the children's programs, pulling weeds together, or helping college students move than they do in your men's or women's ministry? What if your singles study group is really just smearing loneliness around and would be best off re-forming as a weekend breakfast-and-hike group? What if instead of your small group bringing potluck, you actually made dinner together? What if you had a Sunday when you invited all the men over sixty to go do nursery duty together—or just have coffee and chat in the hallway?

I'm not suggesting that worship and prayer be replaced with anything else. But our traditions have tagged some non-prayer, non-worship group activities as holy and others as time wasters. It can be easy to confuse intellectual activities or discussions with spiritual development, when the Bible prescribes hospitality and encouraging each other, among other things. Leaders protect against loneliness when they make group quality time a priority and treat it as a biblically sound use of time.

Develop Place and Hospitality

Psalm 68:6 says, "God sets the lonely in families." This is not a promise but a description of blessing and relief, showing God's character and intentions for humanity. It is now true for some people; someday it will be true for all people. Leaders can influence others' expectations of hospitality by articulating them and practicing them.

Holmer found the verse heartbreaking during a time when she was particularly lonely. "I felt like I did not have a family at that time. I did not have the community that I needed." Holmer's friend, the children's minister, shared that as her favorite verse, prompting Holmer to talk to her more about it. Their relationship became a close one, incorporating Holmer into their family rhythms. "That's exactly what she did for me: her family gave me a family to be in during one of the loneliest parts of my life. I'm incredibly grateful and also still very good friends with her and her family."

Hospitable communities protect against loneliness. Mainstream American culture is very weak when it comes to hospitality. Elsewhere, Christians and non-Christians are eager to have guests and do so as often as they can. I once ate a meal with a family who scraped together a living by shredding carrots. They were so gracious to me that I wouldn't have known how few square meals they got a week if I hadn't known them in another context (and, yes, I brought a big and nutritious hostess gift). That's much closer to biblical hospitality than you'd find in most churches. Americans are more likely to hold off on inviting people over, waiting for coordinated schedules and a chance to do a thorough cleaning. While I applaud clean bathrooms, they are not a biblical virtue, while hospitality emphatically is. Would we be more hospitable if we lowered the stakes and developed skills for welcoming others?

Unmarried people, especially, may find hospitality to be essential if they are to resist loneliness. Stephanie Holmer and Matt Jenson confirm its role in their lives.

Holmer describes something I, too, have done when trying to cultivate a friendship with someone with young children. Holmer thought, "I want to be friends with them. But I know they have two kids and they're stuck at home all the time. And going out to eat is probably not an option. Coming to my house is probably not a great option, because I'm not set up for toddlers." So she brought dinner over to their house. Holmer ended up bringing many meals and forming a deep friendship, helping with the children's bedtime and reading them stories.

When we think of hospitality, we often think of a beautiful and comfortable setting—and we should! Providing a setting for relationships means meeting your guests' wants and needs. Thinking creatively about how to make relationships work can result in everyone enjoying themselves, whether or not the living room is Instagram-perfect. With practice, hospitality becomes a much smaller challenge.

On a different scale, our built environments also should take peoples' wants and needs into account, because our homes and neighborhoods are where relationships happen. Place matters to relationships; neighborhoods matter to loneliness.

Crouch says there was "a watershed moment about 120 years ago where we were realizing we can actually figure out how the world works in a way we never were able to before. So now we can build our dream." It's the wrong dream, Crouch argues. "Part of the dream is isolation," he says. "We built a whole world that would give us that, and it comes down to how our houses are designed."

It's reflected in the proportion of studio apartments in big cities, and in patios instead of porches.[16] "We built the wrong world," Crouch says, "and that's a big part of why we're lonely."

Some leaders will find they will someday have influence on decisions about buildings and design. Likely, it won't happen frequently. We don't even buy houses all that often. But it is still worth considering what to aim for and why.

Offer Practical Help

Leaders can also protect against loneliness by offering practical help and helping others to do the same. It's indirect, but helping with household tasks might be a key part of someone's sense of being isolated, overwhelmed, and unable to invest in relationships.

Driving culture in the United States can play a factor in isolation. For people without licenses, someone who offers a ride, rather than waiting to be asked, can do wonders. Holmer, whose campus ministry includes many foreign students, says they often don't realize at first how difficult it is to do anything without a car. Holmer says, "When students tell me that they don't like Durham, my first question is whether they have a car. A big way to serve international students is by providing transportation. That's a serious relationship builder."

Likewise, Caelene Peake was enormously relieved by her friend helping with groceries and laundry. With a newborn, she was constrained in what she could do and how she could get out. Older adults can have the same trouble.

Conclusion

How can leaders address this epidemic of loneliness? As you've read this book, you've already encountered many of the key elements of avoiding and coming out of loneliness. Here's a summary of ways that leaders can protect against loneliness:

- Not conflating bringing resources to isolated people with addressing loneliness—and yet offering practical help
- Double-checking stereotypes—and yet taking special care to protect people during phases of transition and bereavement
- Inviting people to their homes and encouraging people to host others
- Setting an example of multiple types of close, healthy relationships in which people can find belonging—and

also learning to navigate their disappointment in others and the conflicts that ensue

- Listening and seeking to be reliable—while helping people to make friends with other people
- Offering appropriate physical touch
- Following Jesus in his willingness to be interrupted and to lack privacy—and yet finding counterparts to relax with
- Using norms to others' advantage, emphasizing the majority when the majority is doing something that protects against loneliness
- Giving no oxygen to unreasonable expectations
- Paying attention to the importance of place and jumping at the chance to provide attractive settings for interactions
- Enabling people young and old to get out and about
- Being good neighbors who give others every reason to expect cooperation and friendliness
- Pursuing justice at every level—while learning humbly from those who have been dealing with injustice longer
- Continuing the good traditions of Christian meetings, such as singing, rallying around the work laid out for us in the Bible, and resisting the temptation to dilute meaningfulness
- Helping people deliberately address their loneliness— while helping them resist building relationships as a tactic to meet their own needs
- Not allowing devices to monopolize attention
- Removing the barriers to good marriages—while developing a community that offers emotional intimacy and nurturing relationships to singles

- Questioning their own negative perceptions and expectations of others—and building a foundation for trust and security
- Talking about, rather than tiptoeing around, the emotions people are revealing
- Choosing changes to the post-pandemic balance of digital and in-person interactions carefully—and paying attention to what happens to relationships as they pursue efficiency, attendance, or other values
- Being honest about quick fixes—and being honest about the real comfort to be found in Jesus, Scripture, prayer, existing relationships, and new relationships

Appendix A

WHAT THE BIBLE SAYS ABOUT LONELINESS

Many people who start online searches about loneliness want quotations—and quite often Bible verses. The top Google search for "loneliness" between 2004 and 2020 (that is, a search that someone typed in after searching for loneliness) was for quotations. A search for "loneliness" with "Bible verses" specifically was number seventeen. Clearly, many people interested in loneliness are also wondering what the Bible says about it, and it's safe to assume many of them are experiencing loneliness and looking for comfort.

For better or worse, a word search in the Bible for "lonely" and "loneliness" will yield sparse results; few verses of the day are going to match the experience. Nevertheless, the Bible records a whole lot about loneliness—but it's in the Bible's context. In the sections below, I look at loneliness in the context of the Bible, with a focus on select people from Adam to Jesus.

Should We Feel Lonely?

Many Christians have an idea about loneliness that goes like this: If you feel close to God (as a direct consequence of your devotional life), he will meet all your relationship needs. Wish you had more friends? You don't need them; Jesus will be your friend. Wish you weren't single? Jesus will be your spiritual spouse. Did someone let you down? Jesus will take the sting away.

There's some truth to this, but I want to emphasize that God doesn't always do these things for us when we suffer disappointment. And he certainly doesn't do them because he is compelled by our praying a certain amount or a certain way, or because he has determined that they are the "desires of your heart" (Ps. 37:4). The expectation that we'll get what we want if we just have the right attitude can lead to a lot of suffering and a lot of effort in trying to get God to cooperate with our agendas.

The belief that loneliness is the result of sin doesn't come from the Bible. Don't take my word for it. We can state this belief as a hypothesis—people who are close to God will not feel lonely—and look in the Bible for evidence that disconfirms this idea. What would contradict this statement? A person who is as close as possible to God and yet feels lonely.

Here are a handful of people we know were close to God:

- Adam, who walked and talked with God as a sinless adult and then later as a fallen adult
- Moses, who was so close to God that God's glory rubbed off on him and who had clear, two-way conversations with God as he led the Hebrews out of slavery
- David, twice called a man after God's own heart
- Jesus, God incarnate

Now we look to see if these people were lonely when they were also close to God.

Did Adam feel lonely? The Bible doesn't say so explicitly, but God acknowledges the possibility even in pre-fall Eden. Adam had just named all the animals, but as he named them, he realized none of them were a real match for him. That could mean he started feeling lonely even as he met them all. Then God made Eve, and Adam knew what he had been seeking.

That's an important hint of loneliness, but Adam may have just been at risk of loneliness without experiencing it. Adam's experience might not be enough to convince you that closeness to God can coexist with loneliness.

Did Moses feel lonely? It seems likely. He was caught between his adopted and native cultures as a young man, then ran away from both until old age. His people and his siblings let him down, and his father-in-law seemed the closest thing he had to a friend—and he didn't stick around long. None of this means Moses felt lonely. Perhaps he, Aaron, and Miriam joked around a campfire often and Moses was able to feel all the belonging and closeness he needed—we don't know. But most of us would feel lonely under his circumstances.

David, the second king of Israel as well as a musician, poet, guerrilla, shepherd, and more in his varied career, was close to God—so close that God spoke Scripture through him. We don't have to search hard to find the evidence for David's loneliness—in Psalm 25:16, he says, "I am lonely." Perhaps, though, this was something David experienced when he was not close to God. David is as famous for his dramatic sins as for his good characteristics. Maybe we should keep looking for evidence that people who are close to God can still feel lonely.

Now we come to Jesus, the last person on my list. Jesus isn't just close to God; he is God. There's no concern here that if Jesus felt lonely, it was the result of sin or distance from God. I believe there are multiple scenes in Jesus's life that reveal loneliness. The two most striking are both during his passion.

First, in the garden of Gethsemane, Jesus asks a few of the disciples to keep watch with him. In Matthew 26, he's vulnerable about what he's facing and how much it distresses him, and he asks them to stay with him as his death approaches. They don't; they fall asleep. Jesus complains that they have let him down, asks that they support him, and again returns to find they've conked out. It happens a third time. Who knows what that time with Jesus would have been like if they had supported him? But the evidence we have is that Jesus's friends let him down, and he was hurt by it.

Second, we hear Jesus's cry of loneliness on the cross, "My God, my God, why have you forsaken me?" Of course, it is much more than a cry of loneliness. It is the fulfillment of prophecy and a witness of Jesus's substitutionary atonement. But Jesus's cry isn't less than loneliness. Jesus has been disconnected from the most intimate and important of relationships, and he found the pain of that rejection unbearable.

This is evidence enough that loneliness can coexist with closeness to God. We are prone to loneliness because we were made for relationships, and not only with God. God's design for humans always included deep relationships with other people and other parts of his creation. Loneliness is God's design pushing us toward others, not toward austerity.

Despite having an element of design, loneliness, like other griefs, is mostly with us because of our fallenness. When we are bereaved, betrayed, or let down, we can usually blame humans' choices to sin. Even Jesus's loneliness during his passion was a result of sin, but those sins weren't his own.

Loneliness isn't necessarily linked to our individual sin or our individual closeness to Christ. We can see that righteous people—even the Righteous One—are disappointed in their relationships with other people and even with God.

If our loneliness prompts us to seek God out in prayer and in his Word, it is doing us good. If it prompts us to connect with others, it is doing us good. God is indeed always near to us. But those factors don't always cure or prevent loneliness.

It is time for leaders to stamp out the rumor that a God who designed us for relationships expects us not to hurt over them. He is not only more compassionate than that but he is completely understanding. God's Word knows what loneliness is like.

It's easy to imagine that many, many more of the people following God in the Bible felt loneliness—Mary, with her scandalous pregnancy and her bereavement of husband (we assume) and son; Abraham and Sarah, leaving behind an advanced civilization to camp in the desert; Joseph, a slave elevated in a culture that was grossed out by his rural family business and where he couldn't even eat with others; Noah, preaching repentance to a violent, dying culture; and many more. However, the Bible doesn't record that they expressed the feeling. And while you or I may have struggled with loneliness in their circumstances, it's possible they did not. After all, it's not experiences alone that make a person lonely.

I'd like to walk through a few more of the stories and characters that illustrate aspects of loneliness and God's care of us in loneliness.

Loneliness, Regret, and Rejection: Cain

Cain, the first murderer, does not give the impression of being an intelligent man. He was bitterly angry about God rejecting his sacrifice—so angry he killed his brother out of jealousy. Then God approached him—a hint of God outside Eden I've always wanted to know more about—and confronted him. Cain's sulky evasion did not fool God. Here's the interaction between God and Cain in Genesis 4:9–14:

> Then the Lord said to Cain, "Where is your brother Abel?"
> "I don't know," he replied. "Am I my brother's keeper?"

The LORD said, "What have you done? Listen! Your brother's blood cries out to me from the ground. Now you are under a curse and driven from the ground, which opened its mouth to receive your brother's blood from your hand. When you work the ground, it will no longer yield its crops for you. You will be a restless wanderer on the earth."

Cain said to the LORD, "My punishment is more than I can bear. Today you are driving me from the land, and I will be hidden from your presence; I will be a restless wanderer on the earth, and whoever finds me will kill me."

Cain isn't quoted again. God, in his mercy, doesn't ignore Cain's fear of other people and their sense of . . . is it justice? Or that he'd make a good victim because he was out of God's favor? God puts a mark on Cain and promises dire consequences for anyone who hurts him. It's an unusual sort of exile. Exile as a punishment was often designed to make the exiled person vulnerable. And it would have been just to do so, but God pulled that punch.

It's impossible to know, of course, where Cain's objections were coming from. Was he really in pain over a broken relationship with God? Or did he see God as a sort of protective charm? Since he doesn't apologize, it's likely the latter. Or perhaps he was only objecting to the pain of being cast out.

Cain, like many of us, wanted the results of healthy relationships without having to do anything on his end. I pity his wife and children. Unfortunately, he wasn't the last person to seek out this sort of life.

We can see the consequences of Cain's attitude around us whenever someone wants belonging while abusing others. Such people do tend to find they're shut out of the intimacy that feels best, even when they think they're getting what they want, such as control or respect. One of the consequences of ruining intimacy is loneliness.

Some of us can empathize with Cain. Many more know and love someone who also allows the sin crouching at their doors (Gen. 4:6) to devour them. Their relationships are ruined by fear, jealousy, resentment, addiction, or anger. Sometimes it's a clear choice they made; sometimes not.

The God of the Bible sees and understands such people. He had compassion on Cain, even without Cain in any way indicating he sought godliness.

Dealing with the loneliness in our society will mean helping—not enabling—those in our society who have been the destroyers of intimacy and the violators of neighborliness. I think that means both at the scale of family and friendships and at the scale of prison policy. Just as 2 Corinthians 2:6–8 indicates, we can do too much damage by withdrawing from people for a long time, even if it is necessary for a short time.

For ourselves and others, we can ask for mercy, knowing that just deserts are already taken care of in Christ. After all, if God uses any of us to address loneliness in someone else's life, it will be on the basis of God's righteousness and not anyone else's.

Loneliness and Lament: David

I have seen some of the deserts where David lived in hiding. They look alien and hopeless. If you went down into a valley, you would need the cardiovascular strength of a wolf to get back up. Even in February, you'd get fried like an egg if you didn't cover up, and steamed like a tamale if you did. Those deserts look like places where you'd get lost as soon as you started walking.

David had to run into that landscape, find food and water, and make sure no one reported him to the monomaniacal king. Government officials were pursuing him in order to kill him—and in Psalm 25 he complains about loneliness. Surely it was the least of his troubles?

Yet David's loneliness was a big part of his suffering. In psalm after psalm, David tells God about the pain of rejection and the loneliness of being a political refugee. God listened. We know he listened because he wove David's pain into prophecy and the story of our salvation. It's as if, across time, David and Jesus were singing the same lament together.

Could we—should we—join?

Yes. And we should also learn what aspects of their loneliness we don't participate in.

To get the main difference out of the way, our suffering isn't salvific. Jesus's suffering was. Nor is our suffering a sign that we're not saved, or not sufficiently close to God. That's because our suffering doesn't have to do with our salvation. Nor does our suffering have to do with how close we are to God. We can, however, talk to God about our suffering. That includes loneliness, even when it seems insignificant.

The Psalms often have a transition from praise to complaint, or from complaint to praise. They don't ask us to set aside what's going on in our lives. We have many examples of God honoring the questions of those who turn to him and plead for justice and mercy.

The arts have often been vehicles both for expression of loneliness and for worship. Paintings, poems, and songs can all be stamped with it. After a fairly upbeat era of Christian music, some musicians are writing less simplistic songs. Christian music also includes many spirituals that are laments, in a tradition going back hundreds of years. "Kumbaya," now the butt of jokes about campfire unity, is actually a powerful song asking for God's presence and comfort. "Kumbaya" is a corporate prayer for people in the group who are suffering. It's not a bad example for Christians in our times, especially in contrast to some mistaken ideas of how to handle pain at church.

Linford Detweiler says, "Songs provide the listener a place outside of themselves to store some of those deep feelings that can overwhelm. And the listener becomes part of a bigger narrative, part of a bigger story, where they discover others have been there before them."

Sandra Van Opstal says she's often heard worship leaders say, "No matter what you're going through, no matter what happened this week, just leave that behind you and come and worship God."[1]

"No!" Van Opstal says. "That's the opposite of what Scripture advises us to do. It's *because* of what we've gone through this week, *because* of what we're carrying, *because* we're feeling overwhelmed" that we approach God. When you worship, "bring all that, and cast your anxieties on Jesus. And it doesn't mean forget your anxieties or bypass your anxieties but cast your anxieties on Jesus because he cares."

Van Opstal says that after returning from the US-Mexico border and seeing children who had been separated from their parents, she was so deeply disturbed she was unable to sing with her congregation. "The only thing I could do was weep. And was I participating in worship? Yes. Was I dancing and singing? No." But "what I received was a wave of worship over my back."

For many of us, the "worship"—or singing—portion of church services is a very poor reflection of the worship we have in the Bible. Part of its weakness is the effort to deny the complexity of our emotions in order to worship well, thinking we have to pretend we've sloughed off the pain in our lives as the drums kick in.

Van Opstal sees that many Christian churches overlook the biblical practice of lament. Hopefully, they won't for much longer. "People want to belong where they can come in with all of their feelings. And I believe that the Scripture descriptions do invite us to that. Communal worship is a critical place and space where we experience God's presence in the midst of our anxiety and our fear. And it's a place where our brothers and sisters, who can express their hope and can express their joy, can express that over us."

David was complaining to God about loneliness because he knew God cared. The God who became incarnate as a "man of sorrows" (Isa. 53:3 KJV) doesn't throw people out for insufficient cheerfulness. We, too, can trust that lament has a place in our worship, whether we are alone or together.

Loneliness, Bereavement, and Preemptive Rejection: Naomi

One of the most striking things about living in countries with low Gross Domestic Products is how many people die. I knew a man in East Africa who experienced the deaths of five close family members in the course of eighteen months. A child to a hit-and-run, another child to HIV/AIDS, an uncle to diabetes, an aunt to heart disease, and a brother for reasons I didn't understand. He himself was a candidate for early death from cirrhosis of the liver.

The global death rate has plunged recently.[2] Still, there are many, many widows and orphans, and most live in countries where the government doesn't help to keep them from destitution.[3] So, when the Bible tells us about Naomi losing her husband and two adult children, she may well have been in desperate straits, but her situation couldn't have been rare. Everyone was in desperate straits. There was a famine. We can assume ancient diseases like malaria, cholera, and pneumonia—still top killers today—were picking people off.

There was violence too. The book of Ruth is about people living in the days of the judges, a time when the region plunged into darkness. The Levant experienced a big drop in its city populations during this era, probably from both deaths and migration, and historians have linked these to a mysterious, fierce group known as the Sea Peoples.[4]

Bethlehem may have been too insignificant for raiders to bother with, but surely rumors reached them. Naomi, Ruth, and Orpah suffered enormous losses at a time when many, many other people were suffering. In their region, civilization was collapsing.[5]

And still, Naomi's grief stands out.

When Naomi and Ruth returned to Bethlehem, "the whole town was stirred because of them, and the women exclaimed, 'Can this be Naomi?'" (Ruth 1:19). Presumably, her suffering had changed her. All the conditions of loneliness were there: bereavement, isolation, insecurity, and being a foreigner. Perhaps, since Naomi did not glean along with Ruth, she had some physical disability as well. Even with Ruth, Naomi had been devastated.

Her response to the women in Bethlehem was in keeping with loneliness: "'Don't call me Naomi,' she told them. 'Call me Mara, because the Almighty has made my life very bitter. I went away full, but the LORD has brought me back empty. Why call me Naomi? The LORD has afflicted me; the Almighty has brought misfortune upon me'" (Ruth 1:20–21).

Lonely people demonstrate behaviors of preemptive rejection or withdrawal at a higher rate than unlonely people.[6] I think we can see Naomi demonstrating this. Naomi embraced an identity of bitterness. She told her neighbors it was God's fault. She told her daughters-in-law she had nothing that could make them want to stay with her. She said she was a different person because God had taken away her husband and sons. Like Job, she embodied affliction.

As I write above, I don't believe the Bible ever implies that God generally requires a stiff upper lip. Certainly, he gives us examples of people like David and Job telling him about their pain and makes sure we know they are good examples. Naomi might have done this; we don't know.

But bitterness is bad fruit. The church is warned against bitterness in Ephesians 4:31: "Get rid of all bitterness, rage and anger, brawling and slander, along with every form of malice."

It's listed there among other relationship killers, because bitterness is a relationship killer. It isn't just intense grief but a fault-finding grief that becomes self-perpetuating and all-enveloping.

Naomi seems to have seen the good in releasing her daughters-in-law from their obligations to her, allowing them to remarry and live in a household with a breadwinner who had a better chance at winning bread. That was kindness. But it may also have been withdrawing from the relationships. It sure sounds like Ruth had to convince Naomi to let her stick around.

Naomi had failed to see the good that was left to her because her bitterness had blinded her. In fact, she didn't realize that Ruth could be a breadwinner—or, more accurately, a bread gleaner. Like so many lonely people, she had allowed a filter to be pulled over her eyes so that she saw reasons for mistrust and resentment wherever she looked.

But Naomi didn't end as an old grouch whose bitterness had closed her off from God. She may have been at first, or she may have been intermittently. Naomi was open to change—at least sometimes. She might have announced how disappointed she was in God, but not long afterward Naomi saw God's goodness when Boaz noticed Ruth. She praised God for it: "The Lord bless him!" Naomi said to her daughter-in-law. "He has not stopped showing his kindness to the living and the dead" (Ruth 2:20).

What happened? We'll never know. It may have been sudden or gradual. It might have been a temporary impairment in her perception that lifted. Like many of us when we start resisting loneliness, Naomi may have begun to question her assumption that everything was awful.

If you've read the book, you know that after a wealthy older man jumps at the chance to marry Ruth, Naomi ends up dandling a long-delayed grandchild in their household. God ordered events that gave Naomi belonging and closeness after she was bereaved. He included her in the ancestry of the Messiah. He included her story in the Scriptures.

When we grieve, may we be better than Naomi at resisting bitterness, accepting the love of those who are still close to us, and talking to God about our pain rather than blaming him as its source. But in the end, Naomi is an example to us of someone who got out of a rut of bitterness. When we grieve, may we be like her in praising God's kindness beyond the grave.

Loneliness and Being Let Down: Jesus

In John's Gospel, he tells about one of the Passovers Jesus celebrated in Jerusalem. This time, Jesus draws a lot of attention to himself and makes enemies. He wrecks the vendor stalls in the temple and drives out those selling items for worship. The religious authorities and their followers would have been clamoring for law and order (while understanding Jesus's assertion of his authority) and holding Jesus up as a threat to their culture. But John explains this as the prophesied zeal for God's house consuming the Messiah.

Have you ever expressed zeal and found it to be socially isolating? At certain cultural moments, it has been more acceptable to be ironic, a little upset, to roll our eyes or shake our heads, maybe to curse. In the past few years, however, the sort of zeal that leads to fights seems to be simultaneously the only acceptable response and a completely unacceptable response. I hardly need to refer to the January 2021 attack on the US Capitol by conspiracy theorists, who expected and wanted violent conflict to replace elections. That's zeal, but it's not of Jesus.

Jesus's zeal both drew in and repelled people. Some questioned Jesus's authority and identity; others believed in his name because of his signs.

But Jesus didn't find relief in his new followers. Even those who were already his disciples didn't understand what had happened in the temple until after his death. The Bible says, "But Jesus would not entrust himself to [those who believed in his name when they saw the signs that he was doing], for he knew all people. He did not need any testimony about mankind, for he knew what was in each person" (John 2:24–25).

Jesus knew that people, even people who followed him, weren't trustworthy. He knew this, and yet he loved people. That's a lonely situation.

Jesus knew not only what was in people in general but also—as their Creator—what was in those individuals and what would happen to him in Jerusalem a few Passovers later.

Jesus knew that people's responses to signs have a short half-life. He knew that other pressures and other ways he would fail to meet their hopes and expectations would lead many of them to reject him. He knew that the seed of the gospel was being scattered across all kinds of soils.

Inferring that this made Jesus lonely, as it makes the rest of us lonely, we can see that his loneliness was the result of a real insight into others. Sometimes, this is true of us. Particularly those who have some prominence or status may see that hangers-on are only that and not real friends. Or, worse, we may not see it in time and be let down by the lack of true friendship. After all, belonging takes a sense of mutual love. Jesus, well-loved by his Father and less well-loved by his disciples, was still in a sea of people who would let him be assassinated and would not grasp much at all of what he said about his purpose.

How exhausting! And how human. Jesus understands the isolation that comes with fame, or with others being jealous of you, or with being surrounded by fickle groupies. And yet he didn't reject us. We are those fickle groupies, even those of us who have our own set of fickle groupies.

Jesus's loneliness was part of the suffering he went through for us.

God's Word shows what loneliness is like. Jesus doesn't ask us to deny it or to forgo human-to-human relationships. Instead, he empathizes and cares for us in loneliness.

Appendix B

SHOULD WE LOOK FOR A CURE FOR LONELINESS?

Let's say there was a loneliness pill that led to a loneliness-free happily ever after. If everyone took the pill, no one would ever feel lonely again. Should we do it?

There are plenty of pros. The physical troubles loneliness brings would stop, reducing heart trouble, sleeplessness, memory and thinking problems, and quite possibly other ailments we haven't yet linked to loneliness.

If no one felt lonely, we might find that many people stopped looking to cuddle parties or other forms of intimacy without relationships.

Physicians might stop seeing patients whose main ailment was a lack of company.

Suicides linked to loneliness might go down.

Social media might fuel creativity and appreciation instead of fear of missing out.

People who suffer from injustice might have one less barrier, one less big source of stress.

We might be able to appreciate solitude. We might find that whatever the relationship between privacy and loneliness is, we have a greater capacity for others' company and needs.

Similarly, we might find that the now-mysterious connection between boredom and loneliness means that without loneliness we are less often bored and more able to use our time in ways we like.

But maybe if we got rid of loneliness, it wouldn't be so good after all.

We might not put as much effort into our relationships, ending up contented without confidants to make us wise or intimate friendships to help us enjoy life.

There might be none of the tension and urgency of romance.

We might move farther and farther from each other, literally and figuratively.

Art and music about loneliness would become part of history, as baffling to us as the Old English language. We might start skipping over the Psalms, thinking them a little dangerous for the examples of people complaining to God.

Pros and cons, as many critical thinking experts will tell you, are not a great way to make decisions. That's because they're not the same as income and expenses, where there's a black and a red. One pro (wearing a seatbelt will likely save your life in a car wreck) may outweigh all cons (it takes a few seconds). And some cons (a girlfriend is untrustworthy) can outweigh every pro (she is fun, good-looking, and willing to marry you).

The truth is we don't know what would happen without loneliness. But I don't believe it would be entirely good. Loneliness isn't just a bad feeling that damages our health; it also drives us toward a true need.

I propose a respect and appreciation for loneliness, even as we try to protect ourselves and others from it. First we'll have to work on the stigma many put on loneliness.

Loneliness and the Wholesome Life

Practicing Christians, who attend church monthly and strongly agree that their Christian faith is very important to them, are more likely than other religious groups to stigmatize loneliness. I propose that this stigma is un-Christian. Why? Because of the example of Christ and the content of the Bible. Because it's very dangerous and very common to enforce positivity as a substitute for sanctification. And because it's part of a group of behaviors and situations that aren't normal. I love marriage and think family is of enormous importance. But I worship a God who became incarnate as a single, childless man and who called a single, childless wild man the greatest man on earth (John the Baptist). They lived hard. They died young.

I worship a God who inspired through his Spirit deep cries of loneliness and disappointment, who has allowed people like Job to suffer as much as people can. The sign of the Spirit is not a clean-cut nuclear family and an end to the sense of suffering. No, the joy and peace we have are clearly in all situations, not because of certain approved situations.

C. S. Lewis offers Jesus as an example of someone many churchgoers would bridle at: "He was not at all like the psychologist's picture of the integrated, balanced, adjusted, happily married, employed, popular citizen. You can't really be very well 'adjusted' to your world if it says you 'have a devil' and ends by nailing you up naked to a stake of wood."[1]

God, in fact, blesses negative feelings that are appropriate. We are looking at the dashboard of our lives, and the gauges are all sounding alarms: This is not how it should be! This is unsatisfying! There is injustice! I am lonely! Many people are lonely! To be bothered by these is to point to God's kingdom, and to address these problems can mean cooperating with him.

Two Poems about Marriage

Two poems haunt my thoughts from time to time. They are both about tension in marriage, and they are both about loneliness. They set the couple in different kinds of (metaphorical) containers, alone together. But one is devastating, the other encouraging. The poems are "Modern Love: I" by George Meredith and "The Ache of Marriage" by Denise Levertov. Can you guess from the titles which one is the sadder?

To write about the poems, I have to deflate them a little. Please, go read them completely.

In "Modern Love: I," the speaker (and this does seem to be about Meredith) is in bed with his wife, listening to her try to cry secretly. He moves his hand a little, and "The strange low sobs that shook their common bed / Were called into her with a sharp surprise, / And strangled mute, like little gaping snakes, / Dreadfully venomous to him." Their bed is "their marriage-tomb."

In "The Ache of Marriage," couples are like the animals going up to Noah's ark and like Jonah in the belly of the fish—places where God sent people to be saved from the storms outside. They are there to look for "communion" that is both sex and more than sex. They know that marriage alone has the joy they long for, and yet it's out of reach. So spouses find that the tension of their search for unity nevertheless saves them.

You may find both poems to be sad; you may find all poems to be sad. I happen to like poetry, and I find "The Ache of Marriage" to be gorgeous in multiple senses. Even though it, like "Modern Love: I," is about loneliness and a frustrated desire for unity, the ache in "The Ache of Marriage" is real but healthy. You can see why one couple would be chronically, debilitatingly lonely, and the other would be heading toward a healing, lifelong love. Our responses to loneliness hold us together; our responses to loneliness keep us apart.

Since marriage is a big factor in loneliness, I'll say quickly that anyone promoting marriage as a solution for our society's loneliness epidemic should beware the trap—the tomb—of intimacy without love. "Modern Love: I" warns that marriage is not a solution for each individual or couple. At the same time, "The Ache of Marriage" reflects the truth that a marriage is three strands, as Sharon Hargrave says—I, you, and we.

Beware also romanticizing how marriage, loneliness, and people used to be, and particularly blaming any individual's loneliness on their generation and its worldview. Denise Levertov wrote "The Ache of Marriage" during the height of the sexual revolution in the United States. George Meredith wrote "Modern Love: I" during the height of the Victorian era in England. Who can say whether some of the most healing and beautiful responses to loneliness might come from Gen Z and not from Gen X?

Marriage is significant enough for these poems to be about this topic alone. But, as every Bible reader knows, marriage is big. Marriage is more than marriage as we know it. A marriage will be the culmination of history, and all Christians, no matter our relationship status, will participate.

I believe that many good things will reach their expiration dates at the wedding supper of the Lamb (Rev. 19:9). Hope fulfilled is hope denatured, as Paul points out in Romans 8. So will many of the things that now bring blessing: the dissatisfactions and griefs Jesus blesses in the Beatitudes (Matt. 5:1–12) are not for all time. Nor, it seems, will the blessings of individual marriages and families carry over into eternity in the same way (Matt. 22:30).

Loneliness, too, will be denatured someday as it reaches its telos in unity. We won't be absorbed into one self, but we will find ultimate intimacy. The ark of loneliness is keeping us safely in tension, preserving our desire for the marriage supper of the lamb and keeping us until we know how fully we belong.

NOTES

Chapter 1: Lonely Americans

1. Linford Detweiler, email to the author, October 20, 2020.

2. Detweiler, email to the author.

3. The margin of error is plus or minus 2.9 percentage points at the 95 percent confidence level. OmniPoll is a shared-cost research study Barna conducts at least once a quarter.

4. Barna Group, *The Connected Generation: How Christian Leaders around the World Can Strengthen Faith and Well-Being among 18–35-Year-Olds* (Ventura, CA: Barna Group, 2019).

5. Corresponding to Barna's style, I list in the text only statistics that represent more than seventy-five respondents in the survey results. There are still sound statistical methods of drawing conclusions about patterns (or, so often, of saying that no pattern emerges) with lower numbers of survey respondents, but to avoid confusion, I'll talk about the pattern without talking about the exact proportion in the survey results.

6. Martina Luchetti, Ji Hyun Lee, Damaris Aschwanden, Amanda Sesker, Jason E. Strickhouser, Antonio Terracciano, and Angelina R. Sutin, "The Trajectory of Loneliness in Response to COVID-19," *American Psychologist* 75, no. 7 (2020): 4, https://doi.org/10.1037/amp0000690.

7. Carin Rubenstein and Phillip Shaver, *In Search of Intimacy: Surprising Conclusions from a Nationwide Survey on Loneliness and What to Do about It* (New York: Delacorte, 1982), 2.

8. "TD Bank Survey Finds Many Couples Maintain Separate Bank Accounts," PR Newswire, March 24, 2014, https://www.prnewswire.com/news-releases/td-bank-survey-finds-many-couples-maintain-separate-bank-accounts-251917121.html.

9. Megan Leonhardt, "Separate Bank Accounts Don't Protect You in a Divorce—Here's What Will," CNBC Make It, June 26, 2019, https://www.cnbc.com/2019/06/26/separate-bank-accounts-do-not-protect-you-in-a-divorce-here-is-what-will.html.

10. Miller McPherson, Lynn Smith-Lovin, and Matthew E. Brashears, "Social Isolation in America: Changes in Core Discussion Networks over Two Decades," *American Sociological Review* 71, no. 3 (2006): 358, https://doi.org/10.1177/000312240607100301.

11. Sharon Hargrave, interview with the author, March 2, 2020.

12. McPherson, Smith-Lovin, and Brashears, "Social Isolation in America," 3.

13. Robert D. Putnam, *Bowling Alone: The Collapse and Revival of American Community* (New York: Simon & Schuster, 2000), http://bowlingalone.com/.

14. Cass R. Sunstein, *Conformity: The Power of Social Influences* (New York: New York University Press, 2019), chap 3.

15. John T. Cacioppo, James H. Fowler, and Nicholas A. Christakis, "Alone in the Crowd: The Structure and Spread of Loneliness in a Large Social Network," *Journal of Personality and Social Psychology* 97, no. 6 (2009): 984, https://doi.org/10.1037/a0016076.

16. Daniel Weinstein, Jacques Launay, Eiluned Pearce, Robin I. M. Dunbar, and Lauren Stewart, "Singing and Social Bonding: Changes in Connectivity and Pain Threshold as a Function of Group Size," *Evolution and Human Behavior* 37, no. 2 (2016): 152–58, https://doi.org/10.1016/j.evolhumbehav.2015.10.002.

17. Barna Group, *Households of Faith: The Rituals and Relationships That Turn a Home into a Sacred Space* (Ventura, CA: Barna Group, 2019), 25, 74.

Chapter 2: What Loneliness Is

1. William Wordsworth, "I Wandered Lonely as a Cloud," first published in 1807, available at https://www.poetryfoundation.org/poems/45521/i-wandered-lonely-as-a-cloud.

2. Backstreet Boys, "Show Me the Meaning of Being Lonely," lyrics by Max Martin and Herbie Crichlow, track 3 on *Millennium*, Jive Records, 1999.

3. Online Etymology Dictionary, "lonely" and "loneliness," https://www.etymonline.com/word/lonely and https://www.etymonline.com/word/loneliness.

4. Marilynne Robinson, *Lila* (New York: Farrar, Straus, and Giroux, 2014), 34.

5. Frank Newport, Jeffrey M. Jones, Lydia Saad, and Joseph Carrol, "Americans and Their Pets," Gallup News Service, December 21, 2006, https://news.gallup.com/poll/25969/americans-their-pets.aspx.

6. Louise C. Hawkley and John T. Cacioppo, "Loneliness Matters: A Theoretical and Empirical Review of Consequences and Mechanisms," *Annals*

of *Behavioral Medicine* 40, no. 2 (2010): 218, https://doi.org/10.1007/s12160 -010-9210-8.

7. "Employment by Detailed Occupation, 2019 and Projected 2029," table 1.2, US Bureau of Labor Statistics, September 1, 2020, https://www.bls.gov /emp/tables/emp-by-detailed-occupation.htm.

8. Quoted in Jena McGregor, "This Former Surgeon General Says There's a 'Loneliness Epidemic' and Work Is Partly to Blame," Washington Post, October 4, 2017, https://www.washingtonpost.com/news/on-leadership/wp /2017/10/04/this-former-surgeon-general-says-theres-a-loneliness-epidemic -and-work-is-partly-to-blame/.

9. McGregor, "Former Surgeon General."

10. Charles Eichacker, "8 Deaths Now Tied to Millinocket-Area Wedding Outbreak, Including 7 at Nursing Home," Bangor Daily News, September 19, 2020, https://bangordailynews.com/2020/09/19/news/eight-deaths-now -tied-to-millinocket-area-wedding-outbreak-including-seven-at-nursing -home/.

11. John T. Cacioppo, James H. Fowler, and Nicholas A. Christakis, "Alone in the Crowd: The Structure and Spread of Loneliness in a Large Social Network," *Journal of Personality and Social Psychology* 97, no. 6 (2009): 977–91, https://doi.org/10.1037/a0016076.

12. Cacioppo, Fowler, and Christakis, "Alone in the Crowd," 979.

13. Cacioppo, Fowler, and Christakis, "Alone in the Crowd," 982.

14. Cacioppo, Fowler, and Christakis, "Alone in the Crowd," 986.

15. McGregor, "Former Surgeon General.'"

16. Hawkley and Cacioppo, "Loneliness Matters," 219.

17. Avshalom Caspi, HonaLee Harrington, Terrie E. Moffitt, Barry J. Milne, and Richie Poulton, "Socially Isolated Children 20 Years Later: Risk of Cardiovascular Disease," *Archives of Pediatrics and Adolescent Medicine* 160, no. 8 (2006): 805–11, https://doi.org/10.1001/archpedi.160.8.805; and Cacioppo, Fowler, and Christakis, "Alone in the Crowd," 978.

18. Hawkley and Cacioppo, "Loneliness Matters," 219.

19. National Academies of Sciences, Engineering, and Medicine, *Social Isolation and Loneliness in Older Adults: Opportunities for the Health Care System* (Washington, DC: National Academies Press, 2020), 45, https://doi .org/10.17226/25663.

20. Cacioppo, Fowler, and Christakis, "Alone in the Crowd," 978.

21. Amy Ellis Nutt, "Loneliness Grows from Individual Ache to Public Health Hazard," *Washington Post*, January 31, 2016, https://www.washing tonpost.com/national/health-science/loneliness-grows-from-individual-ache -to-public-health-hazard/2016/01/31/cf246c56-ba20-11e5-99f3-184bc379b12d _story.html.

22. Roy F. Baumeister and Mark R. Leary, "The Need to Belong: Desire for Interpersonal Attachments as a Fundamental Human Motivation," *Psychological Bulletin* 117, no. 3 (1995): 513, https://doi.org/10.1037/0033-2909 .117.3.497.

23. Robert S. Wilson, Kristin R. Krueger, Steven E. Arnold, Julie A. Schneider, Jeremiah F. Kelly, Lisa L. Barnes, Yuxiao Tang, and David A. Bennett, "Loneliness and Risk of Alzheimer Disease," *Archives of General Psychiatry* 64, no. 2 (2007): 234–40, https://doi.org/10.1001/archpsyc.64.2.234.

24. Hawkley and Cacioppo, "Loneliness Matters," 220.

25. Hawkley and Cacioppo, "Loneliness Matters," 219.

26. Wilson et al., "Loneliness and Risk of Alzheimer Disease"; and Cacioppo, Fowler, and Christakis, "Alone in the Crowd."

27. Baumeister and Leary, "Need to Belong" 510.

28. Angus Chen, "Loneliness May Warp Our Genes, and Our Immune Systems," Shots: Health News from NPR, November 29, 2015, https://www.npr.org/sections/health-shots/2015/11/29/457255876/loneliness-may-warp-our-genes-and-our-immune-systems.

29. "Sleep and Sleep Disorders: Data and Statistics," Center for Disease Control and Prevention, May 2, 2017, https://www.cdc.gov/sleep/data_statistics.html.

30. John T. Cacioppo, Louise C. Hawkley, Gary G. Berntson, John M. Ernst, Amber C. Gibbs, Robert Stickgold, and J. Allan Hobson, "Do Lonely Days Invade the Nights? Potential Social Modulation of Sleep Efficiency," *Psychological Science* 13, no. 4 (2002): 384–87, https://journals.sagepub.com/doi/10.1111/1467-9280.00469.

31. Cacioppo, Fowler, and Christakis, "Alone in the Crowd," 985; and Raffaella Calati, Chiara Ferrari, Marie Brittner, Osmano Oasi, Emilie Olié, André F. Carvalho, and Philippe Courtet, "Suicidal Thoughts and Behaviors and Social Isolation: A Narrative Review of the Literature," *Journal of Affective Disorders* (2019): 245.

32. Lisa Jaremka, "Feeling Lonely? Your Brain May Be at Risk," *Psychology Today*, February 22, 2018, https://www.psychologytoday.com/us/blog/the-social-brain/201802/feeling-lonely-your-brain-may-be-risk.

33. Baumeister and Leary, "Need to Belong," 502.

34. Baumeister and Leary, "Need to Belong," 506.

35. Baumeister and Leary, "Need to Belong," 506.

36. Baumeister and Leary, "Need to Belong," 517.

37. Baumeister and Leary, "Need to Belong," 507.

38. Carina J. Gronlund, "Racial and Socioeconomic Disparities in Heat-Related Health Effects and Their Mechanisms: A Review," *Current Epidemiology Reports* 1, no. 3 (2014): 165–73, https://doi.org/10.1007/s40471-014-0014-4.

39. "Marriage and Men's Health," Harvard Health Publishing, July 2010, https://www.health.harvard.edu/mens-health/marriage-and-men-health.

40. Cacioppo, Fowler, and Christakis, "Alone in the Crowd," 977.

41. Caitlin E. Coyle and Elizabeth Dugan, "Social Isolation, Loneliness and Health among Older Adults," *Journal of Aging and Health* 24, no. 8 (2012): 1346, https://doi.org/10.1177/0898264312460275.

42. Coyle and Dugan, "Social Isolation," 1346.

43. The PLOS Genetics Staff, "Correction: The Genetic Correlation between Height and IQ: Shared Genes or Assortative Mating?" PLoS Genetics, March 27, 2014, doi:10.1371/journal.pgen.1004329.

44. Cacioppo, Fowler, and Christakis, "Alone in the Crowd," 977.

45. Marilynne Robinson, *When I Was a Child I Read Books* (New York: Farrar, Straus and Giroux, 2012), 88.

46. Christopher R. Long and James R. Averill, "Solitude: An Exploration of Benefits of Being Alone," *Journal for the Theory of Social Behaviour* (March 5, 2003): 33, https://doi.org/10.1111/1468-5914.00204.

47. Linford Detweiler, email to the author, October 20, 2020.

48. Detweiler, email to the author.

Chapter 3: Age

1. John T. Cacioppo, James H. Fowler, and Nicholas A. Christakis, "Alone in the Crowd: The Structure and Spread of Loneliness in a Large Social Network," *Journal of Personality and Social Psychology* 97, no. 6 (2009): 978, https://doi.org/10.1037/a0016076.

2. Pamela Qualter, Janne Vanhalst, Rebecca Harris, Eeske Van Roekel, Gerine Lodder, Munirah Bangee, Marlies Maes, and Maaike Verhagen, "Loneliness across the Life Span," *Perspectives on Psychological Science* 10, no. 2 (2015): 251, https://doi.org/10.1177/1745691615568999.

3. Jon'athan Vespa, "The Changing Economics and Demographics of Young Adulthood: 1975–2016," United States Census Bureau, April 2017, 4, https://www.census.gov/library/publications/2017/demo/p20-579.html.

4. Vespa, "Changing Economics and Demographics," 4.

5. Brooke Hempell, interview with the author, October 16, 2020. Other observations from Hempell in this chapter are also from this interview.

6. Vespa, "Changing Economics and Demographics," 4.

7. Vespa, "Changing Economics and Demographics," 8.

8. Benjamin Gurrentz, "Living with an Unmarried Partner Now Common for Young Adults," United States Census Bureau, November 15, 2018, https://www.census.gov/library/stories/2018/11/cohabitaiton-is-up-marriage-is-down-for-young-adults.html.

9. Barna Group, *The Generosity Gap: How Christians' Perceptions and Practices of Giving Are Changing—and What It Means for the Church* (Ventura, CA: Barna Group, 2017), 37.

10. Cacioppo, Fowler, and Christakis, "Alone in the Crowd," 978.

11. Richard Fry, Jeffrey S. Passel, and D'Vera Cohn, "A Majority of Young Adults in the U.S. Live with Their Parents for the First Time since the Great Depression," Pew Research Center, September 4, 2020, https://www.pewresearch.org/fact-tank/2020/09/04/a-majority-of-young-adults-in-the-u-s-live-with-their-parents-for-the-first-time-since-the-great-depression/.

12. Vespa, "Changing Economics and Demographics," 15–16.

13. Barna Group, "The Powerful Influence of Moms in Christians' Households," Barna, May 7, 2019, https://www.barna.com/research/moms-chris tians-households/.

14. Jung Choi, Jun Zhu, and Laurie Goodman, *Young Adults Living in Parents' Basements: Causes and Consequences* (Washington, DC: Urban Institute, 2019), 28, https://www.urban.org/sites/default/files/publication/99707 /young_adults_living_in_parents_basements_0.pdf.

15. Jaison R. Abel and Richard Deitz, "Despite Rising Costs, College Is Still a Good Investment," Liberty Street Economics, June 5, 2019, https:// libertystreeteconomics.newyorkfed.org/2019/06/despite-rising-costs-college -is-still-a-good-investment.html.

16. Jean Twenge, "Teens Have Less Face Time with Their Friends—and Are Lonelier Than Ever," The Conversation, March 20, 2019, https://thecon versation.com/teens-have-less-face-time-with-their-friends-and-are-lonelier -than-ever-113240.

17. Sharon Hargrave, interview with the author, March 2, 2020.

18. Qualter et al., "Loneliness across the Life Span," 251.

19. "Mobility Is Most Common Disability among Older Americans," United States Census Bureau, December 2, 2014, https://www.census.gov /newsroom/press-releases/2014/cb14-218.html.

20. "Marital Status of People 15 Years and Over, by Age, Sex, and Personal Earnings: 2019," table A.1, United States Census Bureau, 2019, https://www .census.gov/data/tables/2019/demo/families/cps-2019.html:

21. Ryan Frederick, interview with the author, December 10, 2020.

Chapter 4: Romance

1. Caelene Peake, interview with the author, September 29, 2020. Other observations from Peake in this chapter are also from this interview.

2. Ning Hsieh and Louise Hawkley, "Loneliness in the Older Adult Marriage: Associations with Dyadic Aversion, Indifference, and Ambivalence," *Journal of Social and Personal Relationships* 35, no. 10 (2018): 1301–18, https://doi.org/10.1177/0265407517712480.

3. Roy F. Baumeister and Mark R. Leary, "The Need to Belong: Desire for Interpersonal Attachments as a Fundamental Human Motivation," *Psychological Bulletin* 117, no. 3 (1995): 513, https://doi.org/10.1037/0033-2909 .117.3.497.

4. Pamela Qualter, Janne Vanhalst, Rebecca Harris, Eeske Van Roekel, Gerine Lodder, Munirah Bangee, Marlies Maes, and Maaike Verhagen, "Loneliness across the Life Span," *Perspectives on Psychological Science* 10, no. 2 (2015): 251, https://doi.org/10.1177/1745691615568999.

5. Jeffrey E. Stokes, "Marital Quality and Loneliness in Later Life: A Dyadic Analysis of Older Married Couples in Ireland," *Journal of Social and Personal Relationships* 34, no. 1 (2017): 123, https://doi.org/10.1177 /0265407515626309.

6. John T. Cacioppo, James H. Fowler, and Nicholas A. Christakis, "Alone in the Crowd: The Structure and Spread of Loneliness in a Large Social Network," *Journal of Personality and Social Psychology* 97, no. 6 (2009): 978, https://doi.org/10.1037/a0016076.

7. Matt Jenson, interview with the author, November 23, 2020.

8. Due to rounding, percentages in the figures may total a point above or below 100 percent and may result in slight variations from totals given in the text.

9. Jonathan Vespa, "The Changing Economics and Demographics of Young Adulthood: 1975–2016," United States Census Bureau, April 2017, 4, https://www.census.gov/content/dam/Census/library/publications/2017/demo/p20-579.pdf.

10. "Figure MS-2: Median Age at First Marriage: 1890 to Present," United States Census Bureau, accessed January 5, 2021, https://www.census.gov/content/dam/Census/library/visualizations/time-series/demo/families-and-households/ms-2.pdf.

11. Brooke Hempell, interview with the author, October 16, 2020.

12. Benjamin Gurrentz, "Living with an Unmarried Partner Now Common for Young Adults," United States Census Bureau, November 15, 2018, https://www.census.gov/library/stories/2018/11/cohabitaiton-is-up-marriage-is-down-for-young-adults.html.

13. Nikki Graf, "Key Findings on Marriage and Cohabitation in the U.S.," Pew Research Center, November 6, 2019, https://www.pewresearch.org/fact-tank/2019/11/06/key-findings-on-marriage-and-cohabitation-in-the-u-s/.

14. Graf, "Key Findings."

15. Graf, "Key Findings."

16. "Why Marriage Matters: Thirty Conclusions from the Social Sciences," National Marriage Project, 2012, http://nationalmarriageproject.org/wp-content/uploads/2012/06/WMM_summary.pdf.

17. W. Bradford Wilcox, Jeffrey P. Dew, and Betsy VanDenBerghe, eds., *State of Our Unions 2019: iFidelity: Interactive Technology and Relationship Faithfulness* (National Marriage Project, 2019), 29, http://stateofourunions.org/2019/SOOU2019.pdf.

18. W. Bradford Wilcox and Elizabeth Marquardt, eds., *The State of Our Unions: Marriage in America 2009* (National Marriage Project, 2009), 71, http://www.stateofourunions.org/2009/SOOU2009.pdf.

19. Frank Newport and Joy Wilke, "Most in U.S. Want Marriage, but Its Importance Has Dropped," Gallup, August 2, 2013, https://news.gallup.com/poll/163802/marriage-importance-dropped.aspx.

20. Jenson, interview.

21. Doug Campbell, "Love, Money and Marriage," *Region Focus*, Summer 2006, https://www.richmondfed.org/-/media/richmondfedorg/publications/research/econ_focus/2006/summer/pdf/feature3.pdf; and Abbigail J. Chiodo and Michael T. Owyang, "For Love or Money: Why Married Men Make

More," *Regional Economist*, April 1, 2002, https://www.stlouisfed.org/pub lications/regional-economist/april-2002/for-love-or-money-why-married -men-make-more.

22. Stephanie Holmer, interview with the author, September 11, 2020.

23. "Suicide and Violence Prevention among Gay and Bisexual Men," Centers for Disease Control and Prevention, February 29, 2016, https://www .cdc.gov/msmhealth/suicide-violence-prevention.htm.

24. Frank Newport, "In U.S., Estimate of LGBT Population Rises to 4.5%," Gallup, May 22, 2018, https://news.gallup.com/poll/234863/estimate -lgbt-population-rises.aspx.

Chapter 5: Insecurity

1. John T. Cacioppo, James H. Fowler, and Nicholas A. Christakis, "Alone in the Crowd: The Structure and Spread of Loneliness in a Large Social Network," *Journal of Personality and Social Psychology* 97, no. 6 (2009): 978, https://doi.org/10.1037/a0016076; and Pamela Qualter, Janne Vanhalst, Rebecca Harris, Eeske Van Roekel, Gerine Lodder, Munirah Bangee, Marlies Maes, and Maaike Verhagen, "Loneliness across the Life Span," *Perspectives on Psychological Science* 10, no. 2 (2015): 252–54, https://doi.org/10.1177 /1745691615568999.

2. Kyle Benson, "The Magic Relationship Ratio, According to Science," The Gottman Institute, October 4, 2017, https://www.gottman.com/blog/the -magic-relationship-ratio-according-science/.

3. Roy F. Baumeister and Mark R. Leary, "The Need to Belong: Desire for Interpersonal Attachments as a Fundamental Human Motivation," *Psychological Bulletin* 117, no. 3 (1995): 514, https://doi.org/10.1037/0033-2909 .117.3.497.

4. John D. Harden and Justin Jouvenal, "Crime in U.S. Cities Rose Unevenly after Coronavirus Shutdowns Lifted, with Racial Disparity the Widest in Years," *Washington Post*, October 9, 2020, https://www.washingtonpost .com/graphics/2020/local/public-safety/crime-rate-coronavirus.

5. John T. Cacioppo, James H. Fowler, and Nicholas A. Christakis, "Alone in the Crowd: The Structure and Spread of Loneliness in a Large Social Network," *Journal of Personality and Social Psychology* 97, no. 6 (2009): 978, https://doi.org/10.1037/a0016076.

6. Laura Morosanu, "Between Fragmented Ties and 'Soul Friendships': The Cross-Border Social Connections of Young Romanians in London," *Journal of Ethnic and Migration Studies* 39, no. 3 (2013): 353–72, https:// doi.org/10.1080/1369183X.2013.733858.

7. Sanyin Siang, interview with the author, December 28, 2020.

8. Sandra Van Opstal, interview with the author, November 4, 2020.

9. Thomas Gilovich, Victoria Husted Medvec, and Kenneth Savitsky, "The Spotlight Effect in Social Judgment: An Egocentric Bias in Estimates of the Salience of One's Own Actions and Appearance," *Journal of Personality*

and Social Psychology 78, no. 2 (2000): 211–22, https://doi.org/10.1037/0022 -3514.78.2.211.

10. Sharon Hargrave, interview with the author, March 2, 2020.

11. Qualter et al., "Loneliness across the Life Span," 257.

12. Cacioppo, Fowler, and Christakis, "Alone in the Crowd," 978.

13. Baumeister and Leary, "Need to Belong," 520.

14. Cacioppo, Fowler, and Christakis, "Alone in the Crowd," 978.

15. Louise C. Hawkley and John T. Cacioppo, "Loneliness Matters: A Theoretical and Empirical Review of Consequences and Mechanisms," *Annals of Behavioral Medicine* 40, no. 2 (2010): 220, https://doi.org/10.1007 /s12160-010-9210-8.

16. Hawkley and Cacioppo, "Loneliness Matters," 220.

17. Christopher M. Masi, Hsi Yuan Chen, Louise C. Hawkley, and John T. Cacioppo, "A Meta-Analysis of Interventions to Reduce Loneliness," *Personality and Social Psychology Review* 15, no. 3 (2011): 256, https://doi.org /10.1177/1088868310377394.

18. Masi et al., "Meta-Analysis," 223.

19. Qualter et al., "Loneliness across the Life Span," 258.

20. Masi et al., "Meta-Analysis," 256.

21. David J. Bridgett, Jody M. Ganiban, Jenae M. Neiderhiser, Misaki N. Natsuaki, Daniel S. Shaw, David Reiss, and Leslie D. Leve, "Contributions of Mothers' and Fathers' Parenting to Children's Self-Regulation: Evidence from an Adoption Study," *Developmental Science* 21, no. 6 (2018): e12692, https://doi.org/10.1111/desc.12692.

22. Van Opstal, interview.

23. Baumeister and Leary, "Need to Belong," 508.

Chapter 6: Social Media

1. Chavie Lieber, "Influencer Engagement: How People Can Earn $100,000 per Instagram Post," Vox, November 28, 2018, https://www.vox.com/the -goods/2018/11/28/18116875/influencer-marketing-social-media-engagement -instagram-youtube.

2. Sandra Van Opstal, interview with the author, November 4, 2020.

3. Andrew Perrin and Monica Anderson, "Share of U.S. Adults Using Social Media, Including Facebook, Is Mostly Unchanged since 2018," Pew Research Center, April 10, 2019, https://www.pewresearch.org/fact-tank/2019 /04/10/share-of-u-s-adults-using-social-media-including-facebook-is-mostly -unchanged-since-2018/.

4. Perrin and Anderson, "Share of U.S. Adults Using Social Media."

5. Jean M. Twenge, Brian H. Spitzberg, and W. Keith Campbell, "Less In-Person Social Interaction with Peers among U.S. Adolescents in the 21st Century and Links to Loneliness," *Journal of Social and Personal Relationships* 36, no. 6 (2019): 1903, https://doi.org/10.1177/0265407519836170.

6. Twenge, Spitzberg, and Campbell, "Less In-Person Social Interaction," 1903.

7. Melissa G. Hunt, Rachel Marx, Courtney Lipson, and Jordyn Young, "No More FOMO: Limiting Social Media Decreases Loneliness and Depression," *Journal of Social and Clinical Psychology* 37, no. 10 (2018): 765, https://doi.org/10.1521/jscp.2018.37.10.751.

8. Sharon Hargrave, interview with the author, March 2, 2020.

9. Andy Crouch, interview with the author, November 24, 2020. Other observations from Crouch in this chapter are also from this interview.

10. Hunt et al., "No More FOMO," 763.

11. Brooke Hempell, interview with the author, October 16, 2020. Other observations from Hempell in this chapter are also from this interview.

Chapter 7: Faith and Churchgoing

1. Christopher G. Ellison and Linda K. George, "Religious Involvement, Social Ties, and Social Support in a Southeastern Community," *Journal for the Scientific Study of Religion* 33, no. 1 (1994): 46–61, https://doi.org/10.2307/1386636.

2. Marino A. Bruce, David Martins, Kenrik Duru, Bettina M. Beech, Mario Sims, Nina Harawa, Roberto Vargas, et al., "Church Attendance, Allostatic Load and Mortality in Middle Aged Adults," *PLoS ONE* 12, no. 5 (2017): 9, e0177618, https://doi.org/10.1371/journal.pone.0177618.

3. Julie Zauzmer, "Another Possible Benefit of Going to Church: A 33 Percent Chance of Living Longer," *Washington Post*, May 16, 2016, https://www.washingtonpost.com/news/acts-of-faith/wp/2016/05/16/another-possible-benefit-of-going-to-worship-services-a-33-percent-chance-of-living-longer/.

4. Terrence D. Hill, Reed Deangelis, and Christopher G. Ellison, "Religious Involvement as a Social Determinant of Sleep: An Initial Review and Conceptual Model," *Sleep Health* 4, no. 4 (2018): 325–30, https://doi.org/10.1016/j.sleh.2018.04.001.

5. T. M. Luhrmann, "Why Going to Church Is Good for You," *New York Times*, April 20, 2013, https://www.nytimes.com/2013/04/21/opinion/sunday/luhrmann-why-going-to-church-is-good-for-you.html.

6. Harold G. Koenig, Linda K. George, Judith C. Hays, David B. Larson, Harvey J. Cohen, and Dan G. Blazer, "The Relationship between Religious Activities and Blood Pressure in Older Adults," *International Journal of Psychiatry in Medicine* 28, no. 2 (1998): 189–213, https://doi.org/10.2190/75JM-J234-5JKN-4DQD.

7. Sandra Van Opstal, interview with the author, November 4, 2020. Other observations from Van Opstal in this chapter are also from this interview.

8. Daniel Weinstein, Jacques Launay, Eiluned Pearce, Robin I. Dunbar, and Lauren Stewart, "Singing and Social Bonding: Changes in Connectivity and Pain Threshold as a Function of Group Size," *Evolution and Human Behavior* 37, no. 2 (2016): 152–58, https://doi.org/10.1016/j.evolhumbehav.2015.10.002.

9. Brooke Hempell, interview with the author, October 16, 2020. Other observations from Hempell in this chapter are also from this interview.

10. Barna Group, "Signs of Decline and Hope among Key Metrics of Faith," Barna, March 4, 2020, https://www.barna.com/research/changing -state-of-the-church/.

11. Barna Group, "Signs of Decline and Hope."

12. ACSI and Barna Group, *Multiple Choice: How Parents Sort Education Options in a Changing Market* (Colorado Springs: ACSI, 2017).

13. David Kinnaman and Mark Matlock with Aly Hawkins, *Faith for Exiles: 5 Ways for a New Generation to Follow Jesus* (Grand Rapids: Baker Books, 2019), 33.

Chapter 8: Privacy

1. Derek Thompson, "Why Do American Houses Have So Many Bathrooms?," *Atlantic*, January 23, 2020, https://www.theatlantic.com/ideas/archive /2020/01/why-do-american-houses-have-so-many-bathrooms/605338/.

2. Marieke Heijnen, Oliver Cumming, Rachel Peletz, Gabrielle Ka Seen Chan, Joe Brown, Kelly Baker, and Thomas Clasen, "Shared Sanitation versus Individual Household Latrines: A Systematic Review of Health Outcomes," *PLoS ONE* 9, no. 4 (2014): e93300, https://doi.org/10.1371/journal .pone.0093300.

3. Cass R. Sunstein, *Going to Extremes: How Like Minds Unite and Divide* (New York: Oxford University Press, 2009), 99–127.

4. "Figure HH-4: The Rise of Living Alone," United States Census Bureau, December 2020, https://www.census.gov/content/dam/Census/library /visualizations/time-series/demo/families-and-households/hh-4.pdf.

5. C. S. Lewis, *The Four Loves* (San Francisco: HarperOne, 2017), 7.

6. Keith Dear, Kevin Dutton, and Elaine Fox, "Do 'Watching Eyes' Influence Antisocial Behavior? A Systematic Review & Meta-Analysis," *Evolution and Human Behavior* 40, no. 3 (2019): 277, https://doi.org/10.1016/j.evol humbehav.2019.01.006.

Part 3: Protecting against Loneliness

1. John T. Cacioppo, James H. Fowler, and Nicholas A. Christakis, "Alone in the Crowd: The Structure and Spread of Loneliness in a Large Social Network," *Journal of Personality and Social Psychology* 97, no. 6 (2009): 978, https://doi.org/10.1037/a0016076.

2. Louise C. Hawkley and John T. Cacioppo, "Loneliness Matters: A Theoretical and Empirical Review of Consequences and Mechanisms," *Annals of Behavioral Medicine* 40, no, 2 (2010): 218, https://doi.org/10.1007 /s12160-010-9210-8.

3. Cacioppo, Fowler, and Christakis, "Alone in the Crowd," 982.

Chapter 9: Belonging

1. Roy F. Baumeister and Mark R. Leary, "The Need to Belong: Desire for Interpersonal Attachments as a Fundamental Human Motivation," *Psychological Bulletin* 117, no. 3 (1995): 520, https://doi.org/10.1037/0033-2909.117.3.497.

2. Baumeister and Leary, "Need to Belong," 506.

3. Amy Ellis Nutt, "Loneliness Grows from Individual Ache to Public Health Hazard," *Washington Post*, January 31, 2016, https://www.washington post.com/national/health-science/loneliness-grows-from-individual-ache-to -public-health-hazard/2016/01/31/.

4. Baumeister and Leary, "Need to Belong," 520.

5. Sanyin Siang, interview with the author, December 28, 2020. Other observations from Siang in this chapter are also from this interview.

6. Brooke Hempell, interview with the author, October 16, 2020. Other observations from Hempell in this chapter are also from this interview.

7. Sandra Van Opstal, interview with the author, November 4, 2020. Other observations from Van Opstal in this chapter are also from this interview.

8. This anecdote from Matt Jenson was relayed in an interview with the author, November 23, 2020.

9. John T. Cacioppo, James H. Fowler, and Nicholas A. Christakis, "Alone in the Crowd: The Structure and Spread of Loneliness in a Large Social Network," *Journal of Personality and Social Psychology* 97, no. 6 (2009): 984, https://doi.org/10.1037/a0016076.

10. Cacioppo, Fowler, and Christakis, "Alone in the Crowd," 984.

11. Cacioppo, Fowler, and Christakis, "Alone in the Crowd," 984.

12. Joseph Carroll, "Americans Satisfied with Number of Friends, Closeness of Friendships," Gallup News Service, March 5, 2004, https://news.gallup.com /poll/10891/americans-satisfied-number-friends-closeness-friendships.aspx.

13. Susan Donaldson James, "You Got the Luck of the Irish: You're a Redhead!," ABC News, March 17, 2014, https://abcnews.go.com/Health /redheads-irish-share-lucky-traits/story?id=22916335.

14. Cacioppo, Fowler, and Christakis, "Alone in the Crowd," 983.

15. Cacioppo, Fowler, and Christakis, "Alone in the Crowd," 983.

16. Cacioppo, Fowler, and Christakis, "Alone in the Crowd," 982.

17. Baumeister and Leary, "Need to Belong," 517.

18. Baumeister and Leary, "Need to Belong," 515.

19. Baumeister and Leary, "Need to Belong," 515.

20. Baumeister and Leary, "Need to Belong," 517.

21. David Marmaros and Bruce Sacerdote, "How Do Friendships Form?," *Quarterly Journal of Economics* 121, no. 1 (2006): 94–115, https://doi.org /10.1093/qje/121.1.79.

22. Marmaros and Sacerdote, "How Do Friendships Form?" 94–115.

23. Alan R. Teo, Michael D. Fetters, Kyle Stufflebam, Masaru Tateno, Yatan Balhara, Tae Young Choi, Shigenobu Kanba, Carol A. Mathews, and

Takahiro A. Kato, "Identification of the Hikikomori Syndrome of Social Withdrawal: Psychosocial Features and Treatment Preferences in Four Countries," *International Journal of Social Psychiatry* 61, no. 1 (2015): 64–72, https://doi.org/10.1177/0020764014535758.

24. Melissa Peskin and Fiona N. Newell, "Familiarity Breeds Attraction: Effects of Exposure on the Attractiveness of Typical and Distinctive Faces," *Perception* 33, no. 2 (2004): 148, https://doi.org/10.1068/p5028.

25. Baumeister and Leary, "Need to Belong," 517.

26. Baumeister and Leary, "Need to Belong," 500.

27. C. S. Lewis, *The Four Loves* (San Francisco: HarperOne, 2017), 85.

28. Baumeister and Leary, "Need to Belong," 519.

29. Jenson, interview.

30. Lewis, *Four Loves*, 76.

31. Lewis, *Four Loves*, 77.

32. Tim Keller, Facebook, October 22, 2019, https://www.facebook.com/permalink.php?story_fbid=2707573929282476&id=327083893998170.

33. Sharon Hargrave, interview with the author, March 2, 2020.

Chapter 10: Closeness

1. Stephanie Holmer, interview with the author, September 11, 2020. Other observations from Holmer in this chapter are also from this interview.

2. Liat Ayalon and Inbal Yahav, "Location, Location, Location: Close Ties among Older Continuing Care Retirement Community Residents," *PLoS ONE* 14, no. 11 (2019): e0225554, https://doi.org/10.1371/journal.pone.0225554.

3. Barbara Kafka, *Food for Friends* (New York: Random House, 1984), 2.

4. Barna Group, *Households of Faith: The Rituals and Relationships That Turn a Home into a Sacred Space* (Ventura, CA: Barna Group, 2019), 142.

5. Gary Chapman, *The Five Love Languages: How to Express Heartfelt Commitment to Your Mate* (Chicago: Northfield, 1995), 106.

6. "Can You Kiss and Hug Your Way to Better Health? Research Says Yes," Penn Medicine, January 8, 2018, https://www.pennmedicine.org/updates/blogs/health-and-wellness/2018/february/affection.

7. Roy F. Baumeister and Mark R. Leary, "The Need to Belong: Desire for Interpersonal Attachments as a Fundamental Human Motivation," *Psychological Bulletin* 117, no. 3 (1995): 509, https://doi.org/10.1037/0033-2909.117.3.497.

8. Katie Canales, "What I Learned Cuddling with Strangers at a San Francisco Cuddle Party," *Business Insider*, January 19, 2020, https://www.businessinsider.com/san-francisco-cuddle-party-organized-intimacy-2020-1.

9. Stephanie Pappas, "Oxytocin: Facts about the 'Cuddle Hormone,'" Live Science, June 4, 2015, https://www.livescience.com/42198-what-is-oxytocin.html.

10. Baumeister and Leary, "Need to Belong," 513.

11. Lyman Stone, "Loneliness During the COVID-19 Pandemic," Institute for Family Studies, September 23, 2020, https://ifstudies.org/blog/loneliness-during-the-covid-19-pandemic.

12. John T. Cacioppo, James H. Fowler, and Nicholas A. Christakis, "Alone in the Crowd: The Structure and Spread of Loneliness in a Large Social Network," *Journal of Personality and Social Psychology* 97, no. 6 (2009): 982, https://doi.org/10.1037/a0016076.

13. Ryan Frederick, interview with the author, December 10, 2020. Other observations from Frederick in this chapter are also from this interview.

14. Timothy Matthews, Candice L. Odgers, Andrea Danese, Helen L. Fisher, Joanne B. Newbury, Avshalom Caspi, Terrie E. Moffitt, and Louise Arseneault, "Loneliness and Neighborhood Characteristics: A Multi-informant, Nationally Representative Study of Young Adults," *Psychological Science* 30, no. 5 (2019): 768, https://doi.org/10.1177/0956797619836102.

15. Abigail Murrish, "Porching in Indianapolis," *Comment*, July 3, 2018, https://www.cardus.ca/comment/article/porching-in-indianapolis/.

16. Mona Chalabi, "How Many Times Does the Average Person Move?," FiveThirtyEight, January 29, 2015, https://fivethirtyeight.com/features/how-many-times-the-average-person-moves/.

17. Scott Frickenstein, interview with the author, December 1, 2020.

Chapter 11: Expectations

1. C. S. Lewis, *The Four Loves* (San Francisco: HarperOne, 2017), 3.

2. P. Wesley Schultz, Jessica M. Nolan, Robert B. Cialdini, Noah J. Goldstein, and Vladas Griskevicius, "The Constructive, Destructive, and Reconstructive Power of Social Norms: Research Article," *Psychological Science* 18, no. 5 (2007): 432, https://doi.org/10.1111/j.1467-9280.2007.01917.x.

3. Rich Morin, "Is Divorce Contagious?," Pew Research Center, October 21, 2013, https://www.pewresearch.org/fact-tank/2013/10/21/is-divorce-contagious/.

4. Cass R. Sunstein, "Conformity: The Power of Social Influences," *Social Forces* 99, no. 1 (2020): e11, 79–101, https://doi.org/10.1093/sf/soaa013.

5. Andy Crouch, interview with the author, November 24, 2020. Other observations from Crouch in this chapter are also from this interview.

6. Sharon Hargrave, interview with the author, March 2, 2020.

7. Roy F. Baumeister and Mark R. Leary, "The Need to Belong: Desire for Interpersonal Attachments as a Fundamental Human Motivation," *Psychological Bulletin* 117, no. 3 (1995): 509, https://doi.org/10.1037/0033-2909.117.3.497.

8. Baumeister and Leary, "Need to Belong," 520.

9. Siu Long Lee, Eiluned Pearce, Olesya Ajnakina, Sonia Johnson, Glyn Lewis, Farhana Mann, Alexandra Pitman, et al., "The Association between Loneliness and Depressive Symptoms among Adults Aged 50 Years and Older:

A 12-Year Population-based Cohort Study," *The Lancet Psychiatry* (2020), 55, https: //doi.org/10.1016/S2215-0366(20)30383-7.

10. Zahava Solomon, Mark Waysman, and Mario Mikulincer, "Family Functioning, Perceived Societal Support, and Combat-Related Psychopathology: The Moderating Role of Loneliness," *Journal of Social and Clinical Psychology* 9 (1990): 468, https://doi.org/10.1521/jscp.1990.9.4.456.

11. Baumeister and Leary, "Need to Belong," 521.

12. Randy Rieland, "Can a Pill Fight Loneliness?," *Smithsonian*, February 8, 2019, https://www.smithsonianmag.com/innovation/can-pill-fight-loneliness-180971435/.

13. Chris Harris, "Christmas Loneliness: How Much Solitude Is There across Europe?," Euronews, December 25, 2019, https://www.euronews.com/2019/12/25/christmas-loneliness-how-much-solitude-is-there-across-europe.

14. Marcel Heerink Joost and Henk Rosendal, "Assistive Social Robots in Elderly Care: A Review," *Gerontechnology* 8, no. 2 (2009): 100.

15. Andrew Gilbey and Kawtar Tani, "Companion Animals and Loneliness: A Systematic Review of Quantitative Studies," *Anthrozoos* 28, no. 2 (2015): 181–97, https://doi.org/10.1080/08927936.2015.11435396.

Chapter 12: Breaking the Cycle

1. Katharine Gammon, "Penguins: The Math Behind the Huddle," Inside Science, November 20, 2012, https://www.insidescience.org/news/penguins-math-behind-huddle.

2. Caelene Peake, interview with the author, September 29, 2020. Other observations from Peake in this chapter are also from this interview.

3. Adam Waytz, Eileen Y. Chou, Joe C. Magee, and Adam D. Galinsky, "Not So Lonely at the Top: The Relationship between Power and Loneliness," *Organizational Behavior and Human Decision Processes* 130 (2015): 76, https://doi.org/10.1016/j.obhdp.2015.06.002.

4. Scott Frickenstein, interview with the author, December 1, 2020. Other observations from Frickenstein in this chapter are also from this interview.

5. Andy Crouch, interview with the author, November 24, 2020. Other observations from Crouch in this chapter are also from this interview.

6. Sandra Van Opstal, interview with the author, November 4, 2020. Other observations from Van Opstal in this chapter are also from this interview.

7. Sharon Hargrave, interview with the author, March 2, 2020. Other observations from Hargrave in this chapter are also from this interview.

8. Barna Group, "The Powerful Influence of Moms in Christians' Households," Barna, May 7, 2019, https://www.barna.com/research/moms-christians-households/.

9. Barna Group, *Households of Faith: The Rituals and Relationships That Turn a Home into a Sacred Space* (Ventura, CA: Barna Group, 2019).

10. Jean M. Twenge, Sarah M. Coyne, Jason S. Carroll, and W. Bradford Wilcox, "Teens in Quarantine: Mental Health, Screen Time, and Family

Connection," Institute for Family Studies / Wheatley Institution, 2020, p. 10. Available at ifstudies.org/ifs-admin/resources/final-teenquarantine2020.pdf.

11. Lindsay Favotto, Valerie Michaelson, William Pickett, and Colleen Davison, "The Role of Family and Computer-Mediated Communication in Adolescent Loneliness," *PLoS ONE* 14, no. 6 (2019): 3–8, e0214617, https://doi.org/10.1371/journal.pone.0214617.

12. Brooke Hempell, interview with the author, October 16, 2020. Other observations from Hempell in this chapter are also from this interview.

13. Stephanie Holmer, interview with the author, September 11, 2020. Other observations from Holmer in this chapter are also from this interview.

14. Pamela Qualter, Janne Vanhalst, Rebecca Harris, Eeske Van Roekel, Gerine Lodder, Munirah Bangee, Marlies Maes, and Maaike Verhagen, "Loneliness across the Life Span," *Perspectives on Psychological Science* 10, no. 2 (2015): 259, https://doi.org/10.1177/1745691615568999.

15. Matt Jenson, interview with the author, November 23, 2020.

16. Liat Ayalon and Inbal Yahav, "Location, Location, Location: Close Ties among Older Continuing Care Retirement Community Residents," *PLoS ONE* 14, no. 11 (2019): e0225554, https://doi.org/10.1371/journal.pone.0225554.

Appendix A: What the Bible Says about Loneliness

1. Sandra Van Opstal, interview with the author, November 4, 2020. Other observations from Van Opstal in this appendix are also from this interview.

2. "Death Rate, Crude (per 1,000 People)," World Bank, accessed January 7, 2021, https://data.worldbank.org/indicator/SP.DYN.CDRT.IN.

3. Kasper de Graaf and Risto F. Harma, "The World Widows Report: Statistics," Loomba Foundation, accessed January 7, 2021, https://www.the loombafoundation.org/our-work/research/world-widows-report/statistics; and "Orphan Statistics Explained," Schuster Institute for Investigative Journalism, February 23, 2011, https://www.brandeis.edu/investigate/adoption/orphan-statistics.html.

4. *ESV Study Bible*, "Introduction to Judges" (Wheaton: Crossway, 2007), 434.

5. Joshua J. Mark, "Bronze Age Collapse," Ancient History Encyclopedia, September 20, 2019, https://www.ancient.eu/Bronze_Age_Collapse/.

6. Pamela Qualter, Janne Vanhalst, Rebecca Harris, Eeske Van Roekel, Gerine Lodder, Munirah Bangee, Marlies Maes, and Maaike Verhagen, "Loneliness across the Life Span," *Perspectives on Psychological Science* 10, no. 2 (2015): 260, https://doi.org/10.1177/1745691615568999.

Appendix B: Should We Look for a Cure for Loneliness?

1. C. S. Lewis, *The Four Loves* (London: Geoffrey Bles, 1960), 67.

Susan Mettes (MA, public policy, Duke University) is a behavioral scientist with extensive experience conducting research for faith-based organizations, including Barna Group, Thrivent Financial, and World Vision. She is an associate editor for *Christianity Today* magazine, has written dozens of articles for *CT* and other publications, and is a sought-after speaker. Learn more at susanmettes.com.